OFFICIATING VOLLEYBALL

D1028524

A publication for the National Federation of State High School Associations Officials Education Program

Developed by the American Sport Education Program

Human Kinetics

Library of Congress Cataloging-in-Publication Data

Officiating volleyball / developed by the American Sport Education Program.
    p. cm.
"A publication for the National Federation of State High School Associations Officials Education Program."
Includes index.
ISBN-13: 978-0-7360-5358-7 (soft cover)
ISBN-10: 0-7360-5358-1 (soft cover)
  1. Volleyball--Officiating--United States. 2. Volleyball--Rules. I. American Sport Education Program. II.
National Federation of State High School Associations. Officials Education Program.
GV1015.5.O44O44 2007
796.325--dc22

ISBN-10: 0-7360-5358-1
ISBN-13: 978-0-7360-5358-7

The Web addresses cited in this text were current as of December 2006, unless otherwise noted.

NFHS Officials Education Program Coordinator: Mary Struckhoff; **Project Consultant:** Sheryl Solberg; **Project Writer:** Thomas Hanlon; **Acquisitions Editor:** Emma Sandberg; **Developmental Editor:** Laura Floch; **Assistant Editor:** Cory Weber; **Copyeditor:** Patsy Fortney; **Proofreader:** Bethany Bentley; **Indexers:** Robert and Cynthia Swanson; **Graphic Designer:** Andrew Tietz; **Graphic Artist:** Tara Welsch; **Cover Designer:** Jack W. Davis; **Photographer (cover):** © Columbia Photo, courtesy of the Missouri State High School Activities Association; **Photographer (interior):** © Human Kinetics, unless otherwise noted; **Photo Asset Manager:** Laura Fitch; **Visual Production Assistant:** Joyce Brumfield; **Photo Office Assistant:** Jason Allen; **Art Manager:** Kelly Hendren; **Illustrator:** Argosy; **Printer:** United Graphics

We thank Central Cass High School in Casselton, North Dakota, for assistance in providing the location for the photo shoot for this book.

Copies of this book are available at special discounts for bulk purchase for sales promotions, premiums, fundraising, or educational use. Special editions or book excerpts can also be created to specifications. For details, contact the Special Sales Manager at Human Kinetics.

Printed in the United States of America   10 9 8 7 6 5 4 3 2 1

Human Kinetics
Web site: www.HumanKinetics.com

United States: Human Kinetics
P.O. Box 5076
Champaign, IL 61825-5076
800-747-4457
e-mail: humank@hkusa.com

Canada: Human Kinetics
475 Devonshire Road Unit 100
Windsor, ON N8Y 2L5
800-465-7301 (in Canada only)
e-mail: orders@hkcanada.com

Europe: Human Kinetics
107 Bradford Road
Stanningley
Leeds LS28 6AT, United Kingdom
+44 (0) 113 255 5665
e-mail: hk@hkeurope.com

Australia: Human Kinetics
57A Price Avenue
Lower Mitcham, South Australia 5062
08 8372 0999
e-mail: liaw@hkaustralia.com

New Zealand: Human Kinetics
Division of Sports Distributors NZ Ltd.
P.O. Box 300 226 Albany
North Shore City
Auckland
0064 9 448 1207
e-mail: info@humankinetics.co.nz

CONTENTS

PREFACE

It's no secret that officials are an essential part of volleyball. But how do officials come to know their stuff? How do they keep all the rules and mechanics straight? Educational tools and reference materials—such as this book—help officials not only to learn their craft, but also to stay sharp. *Officiating Volleyball* is a key resource for you if you want to officiate volleyball matches at the high school level. The mechanics you'll find here are those developed by the National Federation of State High School Associations (NFHS) and are used for high school volleyball matches throughout the United States.

We expect that you know at least a little about volleyball, but maybe not much about officiating it. On the other end of the spectrum, you might know lots about the sport *and* how to officiate it. The overall objective of *Officiating Volleyball* is to prepare you to officiate matches, no matter what your level of experience. More specifically, this book should do the following:

- Introduce you to the culture of officiating volleyball
- Tell you what will be expected of you as a volleyball official
- Explain and illustrate in detail the mechanics of officiating the sport
- Show the connection between the rules of the sport and the mechanics of officiating
- Serve as a reference for you throughout your officiating career

Officiating Volleyball covers officiating basics of the sport, officiating mechanics and specific match situations. In Part I you'll read about who volleyball officials are and the qualities you'll find in a good official. Part I also describes the duties of officials, including scorers, timers and line judges. Part II, the meat of the book, explores the prematch, match and postmatch procedures and responsibilities of the referee and umpire, and it describes mechanics in careful detail. Part III highlights some key cases from the *NFHS Case Book*, which will help you apply the rules in action.

NFHS Officials Code of Ethics

Officials at an interscholastic athletic event are participants in the educational development of high school students. As such, they must exercise a high level of self-discipline, independence and responsibility. The purpose of this code is to establish guidelines for ethical standards of conduct for all interscholastic officials.

- Officials shall master both the rules of the game and the mechanics necessary to enforce the rules; they shall exercise authority in an impartial, firm and controlled manner.

- Officials shall work with each other and their state associations in a constructive and cooperative manner.

- Officials shall uphold the honor and dignity of the profession in all interactions with student–athletes, coaches, athletics directors, school administrators, colleagues and the public.

- Officials shall prepare themselves both physically and mentally, shall dress neatly and appropriately and shall comport themselves in a manner consistent with the high standards of the officiating profession.

- Officials shall be punctual and professional in the fulfillment of all contractual obligations.

- Officials shall remain mindful that their conduct influences the respect that student–athletes, coaches and the public hold for the profession.

- Officials shall, while enforcing the rules of play, remain aware of the inherent risk of injury that competition poses to student–athletes. When appropriate, they shall inform event management of conditions or situations that appear unreasonably hazardous.

- Officials shall take reasonable steps to educate themselves about recognizing emergency conditions that might arise during a competition.

KEY TO DIAGRAMS

CB   Center-back player

CF   Center-front player

LB   Left-back player

LF   Left-front player

RB   Right-back player

RF   Right-front player

□   Setter

--→   Player movement

PART I

VOLLEYBALL
OFFICIATING BASICS

CHAPTER 1

INTRODUCTION TO VOLLEYBALL OFFICIATING

In 1895, in a gym in Holyoke, Massachusetts, YMCA instructor William G. Morgan tried out an idea of his on one of his classes of businessmen. Using a tennis net and rules that were inspired from basketball, tennis, baseball and handball, he instructed the men in the first game of what was to become known as volleyball.

Today, nearly 400,000 girls play high school volleyball, and although the participation numbers for boys are low (about 40,000), the combined numbers are exceeded by only five other high school sports. In terms of girls' participation, volleyball ranks third, behind basketball and track and field. Volleyball is popular both above and below the high school level, too: in the United States, 46 million people play the sport at least once a week, and across the world 800 million take to the courts on a regular basis.

Such a popular sport requires high numbers of officials who know the sport, the rules and how to officiate games effectively. Indeed, officiating volleyball is a great way to stay connected to the sport you love. *Officiating Volleyball* will help prepare you to make all the calls while keeping the game where it should be: in the hands of the players.

With that in mind, in this chapter you'll learn about the purpose and philosophy of officiating, who volleyball officials are and what makes a good official, what tools you should use as an official and the basics of officiating volleyball at the high school level. You'll also learn about the role of your state association and the National Federation of State High School Associations (NFHS) in high school volleyball officiating.

Purpose and Philosophy

Your officiating philosophy is an important contributor to your success as an official. How you approach your duties, how you respond to challenging situations and how you continue to learn and apply your knowledge determines, to a significant degree, how much you enjoy being an official and how good you are at it. Know, too, that as you gain experience, situations that were challenging in the beginning will become easier; you'll know how to handle them, and you'll know how to anticipate problems and avoid certain pitfalls or danger areas.

You have three main purposes as an official:

1. To ensure fair play by knowing and upholding the rules of the game.
2. To minimize risks for the players to the extent that you can.
3. To exercise authority in an impartial, firm and controlled manner, as stated in the NFHS Code of Ethics (see page v).

Let's take a moment to consider all three purposes.

Fair Play

Fair play is at the foundation of all games. Nothing will get players, coaches or fans more irate than the belief that the rules are not being applied correctly and fairly. Competitors want and deserve an equal playing field, which requires that officials have excellent knowledge of the rules and that they apply those rules appropriately in all situations.

One of the biggest issues in volleyball, in terms of an equal playing field, is ball-handling calls, particularly with regard to defining the terms *prolonged contact* and *coming to rest* (the ball cannot come to rest or be in prolonged contact with the player's body). Because these terms are somewhat ambiguous, you must rely on your own judgment as to what constitutes prolonged contact and coming to rest. If you aren't consistent in your calls (e.g., calling it tight at times and loose at other times), both teams will be upset with you because they won't know what to expect. Watching established officials work a match will be helpful in setting your own standard of judgment for calling ball handling.

The point essentially is this: To ensure fair play, you have to know the rules and enforce them the same way every time. When you do this, you are on your way to being a good official.

Risk Minimization

Like all sports, volleyball has inherent risks of injury. Two players collide in going for a ball. A blocker twists her ankle as she lands on a teammate's foot after making a block at the net. A passer wrenches his knee as he twists to save an errant pass. The chance for injury is a part of the game. Still, as an official you need to minimize those risks and to respond appropriately when a player is injured. You can do this in four ways:

- Know and enforce the rules. Many of the rules were written to minimize the risk of injury.
- Inspect the court beforehand and report any hazardous conditions to event management.
- Maintain authority and control in all aspects.
- Know how to respond to injuries and emergency situations.

Authority

It's vital that you exercise authority in an impartial, firm and controlled manner. You can know the rules backward and forward, but if you can't exercise your authority, you'll have a difficult time officiating a game.

Everyone involved in the match is looking to you to make the correct calls in a manner that doesn't call extra attention to yourself but shows that you know the rules and know how to apply them fairly. They also need to see that you have control over every situation. If you make calls in an indecisive manner or appear not to know the rules, you are headed for trouble, and it is often difficult to regain authority once you lose it.

To gain and maintain authority, you must be decisive and consistent in your calls, retain control at all times and make impartial calls. When you do this, you not only maintain your authority, but also uphold the honor and dignity of the profession. Coaches and players prefer to have games called by officials who maintain consistent authority because they know what to expect from such officials. This doesn't mean that you never make a mistake; it means that you never lose control of the game. Part of maintaining control comes from knowing the rules.

Who Are Volleyball Officials?

Volleyball officials come from all walks of life—teachers, accountants, small business owners, postal workers, and on and on. Some have played high school or college volleyball; others have played, and continue to play, recreationally. Some are just out of high school; others are approaching or are into retirement.

Despite these differences, good officials have much in common. They are critical thinkers who can make decisions in the heat of the moment while maintaining poise. They are peacekeepers and negotiators. They know when and how to stroke an ego without demeaning themselves or harming the integrity of the game. They know when and how to sell a call. They have thick skins and a great deal of patience.

The common denominator, it seems, for all volleyball officials is their love for the sport. In many cases, officials are giving back to a sport that has given so much to them. Being an official is a great way to give back to a sport, to help a sport continue and flourish and to play an integral role in the enjoyment of the sport by athletes, coaches and fans alike.

What Makes a Good Volleyball Official?

Just as players need a mix of skills to be good players, officials need a range of skills and competencies to be good officials. You need a combination of qualities, some of which you probably already have. Others you'll develop over time as you gain experience. The same personality traits that make a successful supervisor or director make a successful official. Attention to detail, alertness and quick but sound reactions are qualities that you must cultivate. Characteristics that distinguish exceptional officiating from average officiating include confidence, decisiveness, courage, mental toughness, good instincts and resolve.

Expectations for officials are high. Your role on the court is similar to that of a school principal or a police officer. You are expected to be the authority at all times, restoring order in some of the most tenuous circumstances. Fans, coaches and players may not always hold you in the highest regard, but they still count on you for fairness and professionalism at all times.

Like athletes, officials are expected to improve their skills. And like players, officials need a range of skills to excel. Sometimes those skills can seem almost contradictory. For example, to be a good official, you have to maintain control of the game yet ensure that the game remains in the players' hands. While the emotions around you fly high, you must remain calm and collected at all times.

You will make mistakes. No one is perfect. Don't be too hard on yourself; simply learn from your mistakes and do your best not to repeat them. Becoming a good official is not easy. It takes commitment, dedication and preparation. You can join the ranks of good officials by following the eight prerequisites for good officiating.

1. Know the rules.

Rules competence comes from study, preparation and experience. The rules are one of your most useful tools. Because you make some decisions more often than others, you'll find that those calls will soon come naturally. Through continual study of different situations, you'll be prepared to make any call.

It's one thing to know the rules, however, and quite another to apply them during a match. As you study the rules, visualize plays. These images will allow you to recognize situations when they occur during games, helping you to make the correct calls with confidence. Remember, if you don't make your calls confidently, fans, players and coaches will assume that you don't know the rules and they will lose respect for you.

2. Master the mechanics.

Your knowledge of the rules might be extensive and your command of the language impressive, but if your mechanics are poor, you will have a hard time getting your calls accepted and administering a match. Observe other officials' techniques and continue to hone your own signaling skills. Be aware of the entire court (not just the ball), know which calls are yours to make, and make them.

3. Make calls positively and with good timing.

Your positive and forceful action does much in getting your call accepted. Timidity or extended hesitation indicates a lack of confidence. Cultivate your voice to increase your authority, and make all calls distinctly and clearly so that players of both teams can hear them.

If you're a novice official, be careful about rendering decisions prematurely, but also don't be too hasty in calling a play. For example, call an illegal back-row attack only after the ball has crossed the net or is legally blocked by the opponent, and make sure a net foul has occurred (did just the player's hair touch the net, or did a part of her body?) before making the call.

4. Focus on the court, not the stands.

Be prepared for heckling. Every crowd includes fans who live to insult and distract the officials. You must ignore them. Reacting to fans will never serve you well and will only detract from your ability to call the game. If fans sense that they can get to you, their heckling will only increase. Tune out fans and stay focused on the action.

Your job is to make the right call at the right time. Even if fans, players or coaches become irate, you should maintain a calm demeanor, staying away from anger and frustration. You are counted on to keep the game's temperature under control. Enlist the help of your fellow officials in potentially volatile situations, and be prepared to handle such situations.

5. Be professional.

Gain the respect of coaches, athletes and other officials by being ethical, fair and honest, conforming to the code of ethics shown on page v. Approach each contest the same way, giving it your very best regardless of level or status.

It's OK to be friendly toward players and coaches and other personnel, but avoid visiting excessively with them (other than game management personnel) immediately before, during or after a match. Additionally, don't argue with players, coaches or team representatives. Never get emotionally involved. Be courteous, tactful and polite, but don't back down on decisions or rulings that you make. A professional attitude will often defuse a problem should one arise.

On a similar note, your personal appearance counts (see "Official's Uniform and Equipment"). When you look clean and sharp and your uniform is pressed and in good repair, you send a professional message to others.

6. Stay in shape.

Although you don't have to be in great physical shape to officiate volleyball, being healthy and fit is better for you personally, and it presents a better image to those around you. Better conditioning also helps you maintain your energy level and alertness throughout a match.

7. Expand your knowledge.

Although it's essential that you know the rules, your knowledge doesn't begin and end with the rules. It expands as you gain experience, as you face and handle difficult or unusual situations, as you deal with all types of personalities on the court, as you learn the intricacies of the game and as you gain confidence in your ability to officiate at all levels of high school play. This expansion comes through actual experience, through observing veteran officials and talking with them, through reading and through clinics, for starters. The point is, good officials don't rest on their laurels. They keep improving, keep expanding their knowledge and expertise.

8. Be passionate about officiating.

Without a passion for the game and for officiating, you will have difficulty becoming a great volleyball official. When you bring energy and enthusiasm to your officiating, you're more likely to succeed. The more you give, the more you get back in return.

Do all you can to contribute to or maintain the traditions of volleyball; give your chosen avocation the best possible service. Carry out your assignments to the best of your ability, and maintain your integrity at all times.

Official's Uniform and Equipment

As a high school volleyball official, keep in mind that you have only one chance to make a first impression. Your appearance is important in beginning the match on a positive and professional note. Following is specific information about a volleyball official's proper uniform and equipment.

Uniform

A volleyball official's uniform should be neat and clean, should be of proper size and should not be loose or ill-fitting. Following is detailed information about each piece of your uniform.

- *Shirt.* The shirt must be an all-white collared polo shirt and should be tucked in. The proper prescribed state association official's patch should be displayed in the location determined by your state association.
- *Pants.* Pants must be a crisp black and should be replaced if they become faded with use.
- *Jacket.* Jackets are optional depending on the weather, but if you wear a jacket before the match, it is recommended that it be black. Check with your state association or local officials association because they may have a specific jacket available for purchase.
- *Shoes.* Shoes should be comfortable, supportive solid black athletic shoes and should be kept shined. Avoid street or high-fashion shoes or shoes that have decorations such as colored stripes or logos that detract from your clean and crisp appearance.
- *Socks.* Socks should be black and comfortable and should be replaced if they become faded with use.

Equipment

Whether you are a volleyball referee or umpire, you should have the following equipment with you at all times:

- Two whistles on lanyards (black is ideal)
- Coin (avoid using comical coins in an effort to maintain professionalism in the sport)
- Umpire's lineup card
- Two pens or pencils
- Set of red and yellow cards
- Tape measure to measure the net (Although the home management should supply a tape measure, it is wise to have one in your officiating bag.)
- Ball gauge
- Watch or timing device

Officiating at the High School Level

Officiating volleyball at the high school level is similar to officiating at levels that are lower and higher, but some aspects make the high school experience unique.

At youth levels, officials sometimes coach the players, giving them technique tips or allowing them to bend the rules as they learn the game. This does not happen at the high school level; rather, you simply call the game fairly and authoritatively.

You also might have officiated in various types of tournaments or matches: mixed-six (coed); reverse mixed-six; beach; indoor; outdoor; and in games using two, three, four or six players per side. Rule variations abound, and net heights differ based on gender, age and competition levels. The focus of this book is on the high school game, using the NFHS rules.

There are two points to remember at the high school level. First, rules change. Keep up with them, know them and know how to apply them. Second, if you've officiated at a different level, make sure you are well versed in the high school rules and the officiating philosophy of that level of play. These should guide your approach to the game.

Officiating at the high school level involves many factors, including licensing, receiving assignments, signing contracts, filing reports, securing insurance and other matters. Let's take a look at these factors more closely.

Licensing

You must be licensed or certified by your state association to officiate volleyball. You also are required to register with your state association and follow their guidelines. The association will provide you with the necessary rules books, supplements and state policy information. These associations have rating systems or classification procedures for officials; make every effort to move toward the highest classification. The bottom line is that you need to possess the skills and knowledge necessary for officiating volleyball and demonstrate the same exemplary behavior expected of officials in all sports.

Receiving Assignments

Assignments can come from a variety of sources, including your state association, your local or state officials' association, leagues or conference commissioners or assigners and local athletic administrators. Keep a schedule book, and be sure to respond to date requests immediately. Belonging to a local as well as a state officials association will help you

Volleyball Official's Tools

Use the following tools to help you learn and grow as an official:

- *The current* NFHS Volleyball Rules Book. Get it and learn it backward and forward.
- *The current* NFHS Case Book and Officials Manual. This provides play situations and rulings along with a review of officiating mechanics.
- *Officiating resources.* To hone your skills, use this book and the *Officiating Volleyball* CD-ROM, which shows animated mechanics, as well as books, magazines and other resources.
- *Firsthand experience.* Use every officiating experience to improve your ability to officiate and expand your knowledge of the game.
- *Secondhand experience.* Learn from watching good officials, either in person or on tape. Check out their mechanics, how they comport themselves, how they exercise authority, how they deal with coaches and players and how they make their calls. Learn from their experience and style and adapt what you observe to your own style.
- *Clinics and workshops.* Attend as many rules seminars as possible. If none are offered in your area, contact veteran officials and recommend that they design one of their own. Call your local schools or recreational organizations about developing workshops.
- *Journal.* Keep a journal as a self-assessment tool, charting areas for improvement, successes, progress and things you learned from each match.
- *Self-review.* Hire someone or have a friend record your games so that you can track your progress over the season. Recordings of games can be excellent learning tools.
- *Feedback from others.* Invite feedback by asking fellow officials to watch you and comment on your work.
- *Pre- and postmatch meetings.* Meetings before and after matches are key learning times for officials, especially beginners. Don't be afraid to admit you don't know something or you need help.

garner assignments. In volleyball, some states require that you join a local association, which assigns matches. Usually, the local association requires some type of membership fee; in turn, the association represents you and works with the schools in the area to make officiating assignments. In other states you may have the option of joining an association, or you may act as an independent contractor and directly contact the coach or athletic administrator of each school.

Understand that if you're a new official, it can take a while to break into the system and receive a full load of assignments. Be patient, don't shy away from doing junior high or freshman or JV matches and keep working at improving your skills as you gain more and more matches. Although working the big match at the powerhouse high school might sound nice, receiving such an assignment could have a detrimental effect on your officiating career if you're not ready for it. Officiating a sport mirrors playing one: You have to work your way up and prepare yourself for prime time.

Contracts, Reports and Insurance

All match contracts and agreements should be put in writing to avoid any misunderstanding as to terms and dates. You might consider retaining the services of an attorney to make sure all written agreements are legally sound. Many state officials associations and state high school associations provide sample contract forms, so check with these organizations.

Using agreements promotes professionalism and organization. It can also assist with essential record keeping come tax season. What might appear to be a straightforward officiating deal should still be committed to paper. Be prompt and professional in making or responding to requests. Here are a few things to remember about setting up matches and keeping records:

1. Always confirm the date, time and location of the match in writing. If you need directions to the location, don't hesitate to ask.

2. About a week before the contest, send a note to the contest manager confirming your participation.

3. File all pertinent agreements and documents, including appropriate receipts and vouchers.

Because most associations require some form of reporting, be sure to submit all paperwork promptly. If you are unclear about something related to the report, call the association. If rating reports are used, send them. As an important part of maintaining the sport's integrity, you are required to report any unusual or unsporting behavior. Do so, and be ready to provide testimony if called upon.

Additionally, if your state association or officials association does not provide insurance, it's your responsibility to secure any coverage that you desire.

We've mentioned several ways to grow and develop as an official: by expanding your knowledge, gaining experience, attending clinics, learning from veteran officials, and so on. You can also grow and develop through your membership with the NFHS Officials Association and with your state officials association.

The first part of that growth is through this book and through the online course for which this book is the text. (If you're not already registered for the course, visit www.ASEP.com to find out how to register.) But that's the beginning of your growth, not the end. The NFHS and your state officials association can help you grow in a number of ways, through publications, meetings, clinics and workshops, and so on. Take advantage of your membership in these organizations to continue to learn and develop your skills as an official.

Now that you've been introduced to some of the foundational elements of volleyball officiating, let's move on to more specifics. In the next chapter we'll explore the duties of officials.

CHAPTER 2

Duties of Volleyball Officials

The officiating crew for a volleyball match consists of a referee, an umpire, a scorer, an assistant scorer (libero tracker), a timer and two line judges. In this chapter we examine the duties of each official. We only briefly introduce the referee's and umpire's roles, because we will explore match procedures and the referee's and umpire's responsibilities further in chapter 3.

Referee

As the referee, you are the head official in charge of all other officials. You are on an elevated platform at the end of the net, opposite the officials' table, with your head 2 to 3 feet above the net (as shown in figure 2.1) so you have an unobstructed view of both playing areas of the court. Your specific duties are spelled out in the next chapter, but know that you are the official who decides matters not specifically covered in the rules, and who makes the final decision when a disagreement occurs between officials.

Refereeing takes great observation skills. When you can combine superior observation skills with anticipation of play, you're on your way to being a top-notch referee. One of the most common mistakes inexperienced referees make is falling victim to "tunnel vision" and continuously focusing on the ball. Although this may seem like a good thing to do because, after all, the ball is of critical importance in every play, referees must learn that the ball, and the players in the immediate vicinity of the ball, actually constitute only part of the action. To become a strong referee, you should develop the following observation skills:

- *Maintain an open view.* You maintain an open view by using peripheral vision, being aware of what's going on beyond the ball and avoiding being screened by players, the pole, the pad or the net.

FIGURE 2.1   Referee positioning.

Doing this allows you to cover your immediate responsibility and also gain important information beyond that. Keeping your eye on the surrounding developments helps you to anticipate the action and be ready to make the call.

- *Scan the court and surrounding area.* When you scan, you should scan more than just the court. Before the serve you should scan from wall to wall, taking in the umpire, line judges, benches, scorer and timer, and teams. Once play begins, scan from line judge to line judge, including off-court areas that are playable.

- *Make wise use of your time.* Making wise use of your time refers to knowing when to scan. Although volleyball is a fast-paced game, there are free times even during a rally to scan the court quickly, and there are pauses during the game to scan more completely. Doing so will help you fulfill your duties and be prepared for anything that comes up.

Umpire

The umpire assists the referee in prematch, match and postmatch duties, which are described in detail in the next chapter. As umpire, you stand on the floor opposite the referee, outside the sideline boundary and back from the standard (see figure 2.2). Play around the net and the center line is the umpire's primary concern.

In addition to knowing the rules and proper mechanics, you'll be well served to maintain your poise, composure and alertness at all times during a match. As is the case with the referee, make sure you constantly scan the court, not focusing solely on the ball. Listening to the sounds coming from the court and the benches will also help inform you of potential problems. You should also keep checking in visually with the referee, the line judges and the coaches, and listen for the scorers. For more information on communicating with the referee, see "Communication and Interaction Among Officials" on page 19.

Scorer

The essential duties of the scorer include keeping track of the serving order, scoring the games, noting penalties and recording comments in the scoresheet, correcting the score when necessary and recording substitutions. The scorer also notifies the umpire when a team reaches game point.

The scorer and assistant scorer should report to the referee at least 20 minutes before the scheduled starting time of the match. The scorer should be equipped with a scorebook (the *NFHS Official Volleyball Scorebook* is strongly recommended) and pens or pencils of two different colors. As

FIGURE 2.2   Umpire positioning.

shown in the sample scoresheet in figure 2.3, you will need to complete the match information section, leaving blank the spaces provided for the referee's initials and the final outcome of the match. Although you record the score, the umpire confirms the score after each game by checking the score and initialing the scoresheet. The referee initials the scoresheet at the end of the match. Once the referee verifies the scoresheet at the end of the match, the match is official and no changes can be made to the sheet. A visible scoreboard should be available so that the score can be viewed.

Each square across the scoresheet, unless otherwise indicated, represents a serve (the squares are also used to record substitutions and timeouts, as explained later). As the scorer, you will need to record each play, using the appropriate figure as shown at the bottom of figure 2.3.

Also remember that we suggested that you bring pens or pencils of two different colors. This is so you can record each complete rotation of service in alternating colors.

DATE: __10/22__ HOME: __Wilson__ VISITOR: __Newton__ SITE: __Wilson__ START TIME: __7:30 p.m.__ END TIME: __8:01 p.m.__

Game No. 1	TIME-OUTS			
	8-5	9-12		L __2__

Serve Order	Player No.	Team: Newton																					
1	5	△	△	△	T	20	T																
2	4	4	R	5	6	5×13	7	8	P1	21	22												
			Tx	23	24																		
3	3 13 3	9	T	25	T		T																
4	12c	10	11	12	13		T																
5	11	14	5×13	15	5×33 21		T																
6	10	16	17	18	19	RS	RS																

Comments: R=3(8-1),Y=1 2(8-8),R=1 2(9-1 1)

Subs: 1 2 3 4 5 6 7 8 9 10 11 12 13 14 15 16 17 18
Referee: ____

First Serve (check box below)			
X			
	16	1	16
	17	P2	17
	18	3	18
	19	4	19
	20	5	20
	21	6	21
	22	7	22
	23	8	23
	24	9	24
	25	10	25
	26	11	26
	27	12	27
	28	13	28
	29	14	29
	30	15	30
Final Score:	25		27

Game No. 1	TIME-OUTS	
	21-22	

Serve Order	Player No.	Team: Wilson																						
1	13 5	1	T	20	21		T																	
2	14c	2	3	4	5	P25	Tx	5×13	6	7	8	T												
		22	23	24																				
3	15	9	10	11	RS	P12	Tx	13	T	26	27													
4	20	14	T			T																		
5	21 33	5	16	17	18	T																		
6	22	19	T																					

Comments:

Subs: 1 2 3 4 5 6 7 8 9 10 11 12 13 14 15 16 17 18
Umpire: ____

Official Verification __SS__

Key: c = Playing Captain   1 = Point   ⊣ = Loss of Rally   P = Penalty
R = Replay   RS = Re-Serve
S = Substitution   Sx = Substitution Opponent   T = Time-out   Tx = Time-out Opponent
T = Time-out Opponent   △ = Libero Service

FIGURE 2.3   Sample scoresheet showing match information.

Communication and Interaction Among Officials

Communication is the key to success for officiating crews. That communication begins in the prematch conference, when responsibilities are discussed, and continues throughout the match. Following are some tips for good communication:

- *Maintain eye contact throughout the match.* Line judges should look at the referee when making a call; the referee and umpire should be making constant visual contact with each other before serves and between plays.
- *Provide complete information.* Both verbally and through signals, you need to communicate clearly and completely with your fellow officials. For example, if a ball is spiked into a block and goes out, signify not just that the ball went out, but on whom.
- *Support your fellow officials.* Don't openly question another official's call when that call is made within his or her outlined duties. Don't override fellow officials' decisions (unless you are the head referee overruling another official).
- *Work as a team.* Just as players work as a team, so should officials. Although both the referee and the umpire have the responsibility of scanning the entire court, if the umpire sees the referee scanning one way, he or she should scan the other way. If you're both watching the same thing or the same area, you might be missing something important elsewhere.

In the rest of this section we'll detail your prematch and match duties as the scorer.

Prematch Duties

At least 10 minutes before the end of the prematch warm-up, you should receive a written, accurate team roster from each coach. Keep these rosters with your official scoresheet. No later than 2 minutes before the end of the prematch warm-up, you must receive a written, accurate numeric lineup listing the serve order for the first game from each coach. For subsequent games, you should receive starting lineups in serve order at least 1 minute before the end of the intermission period. If you don't receive the lineups by this time, you should inform the umpire or referee.

When you receive the starting lineups, in the "Player No." column, record on the game scoresheet the numbers of the players of each team in the serving order submitted by the coach at the beginning of the

Assistant Scorer (Libero Tracker)

If at least one team is using a libero player—a player who may replace any back-row player for the purpose of playing defense—your officiating crew will have an assistant scorer. The assistant scorer is positioned at the score table next to the scorer and is responsible for tracking libero replacements and substitutions. Also record the serving order in which the libero serves, if applicable.

Before the start of the game, when the scorer receives the starting lineups, the assistant scorer is responsible for recording on the tracking sheet the numbers of the players of each team in the serving order for that game.

As the game progresses, the assistant scorer records all substitutions and replacements, making sure the player the libero replaces is the same player that will come back into the game to replace the libero. For example, assume that the starting CB player #3 is replaced by the libero. When the libero is replaced, it must be the same player (#3). The assistant scorer must notify the umpire during the first dead ball if there is a discrepancy with a replacement. The assistant scorer must notify the scorer to sound a signal at the time the ball is contacted for the serve when there is an illegal replacement.

game (figure 2.3 on page 18 shows a completed "Player No." column). It is also good preventive officiating for the umpire to check with the coach to see whether a libero player will be used if it is not marked on the lineup sheet.

Match Duties

During a match, you should refrain from socializing with spectators or others, because your duties will require your entire concentration. Given the speed of the game, you will need to be focused solely on the action so that you can properly record the scoring, keep track of the serving order and substitutions and note penalties and comments. These and similar duties are your primary match responsibilities.

Serving Order   Based on the lineups submitted prior to the game, you know the serving order for each team. As the game progresses, track the order and make sure that each player is taking her or his proper turn. If someone serves out of turn, you should instruct the timer to sound the horn and notify the umpire or referee as soon as the server contacts the ball. Also, if the libero serves in one of the six serving rotations, mark this on the scoresheet with a triangle (as shown in figure 2.3 on page 18) and make sure the libero only serves in that rotation for the remainder of the game.

Keeping Score   Keep the scoresheet with you at the officials' table at all times throughout the match, and use it only to keep score; don't use it to keep any other individual or team statistics. You'll remain the scorer throughout the match unless you prove to be incompetent. The referee has the authority to remove a scorer who, in his or her opinion, is not performing the job properly.

After each rally, record the individual and team point in the squares on the scoresheet (see figure 2.3 on page 18 for an example of a completed scoresheet), and then update, or supervise the updating of, the scoreboard.

Recording Comments   Another aspect of the scorer's duties is to record comments regarding penalties and cards issued in the comment section on the scoresheet (the comments section is at the bottom of the scoresheet, as you can see in figure 2.3 on page 18). Use the comments section to record penalties for illegal uniform or equipment, exceptional substitution, red and yellow cards and unconscious or apparently unconscious players.

Here are some examples of how you should record comments for various situations:

- *Y #12 (7-6).* This means that a yellow warning card was issued to player #12 when the score was 7 to 6 (always list the score of the offending player's team first). Use this procedure for a coach or any player on the bench.
- *R #3 (7-0).* This means that a red penalty card was issued to player #3 when her team was ahead 7 to 0.
- *DQ #10 (4-14).* This means that player #10 was disqualified (yellow and red cards were held apart) when his team trailed 4 to 14.
- *E #10 (3-0).* This means that there was an equipment or uniform violation. Player #10 entered, or attempted to enter, the game while wearing illegal equipment or an illegal uniform.
- *Unconscious player #8.* This means that player #8 was deemed unconscious. Note this any time an unconscious, or apparently unconscious, player has been removed from the game.
- *ExS #20.* This means that player #20 has been replaced by an exceptional substitution. This typically occurs when a team has exhausted its team substitutions or when no legal substitutes are available and a player on the court is ill or injured.

Correcting the Score   Scorers sometimes need to correct a score. For example, if the score on your scoresheet does not coincide with the score on the scoreboard, or if the individual score and the team score on your scoresheet do not jive, you need to correct the error. Notify the umpire during the first dead ball after you notice the error, and then, with the supervision of the umpire if needed, correct the score.

If the team score on the scoresheet is less than the individuals' combined scores, you should correct this immediately (making the team score the same as the combined total of the individuals' scores). If the team score is higher than the individuals' combined scores, again adjust the team score to match the individual scores. If you can't determine where the error lies—with the individuals' combined scores or with the team score—consider the individual scores to be correct.

Recording Substitutions   Another duty, as the scorer, is to record the substitutions that each team makes as they are reported by the umpire (see figure 2.3 on page 18 for a completed example of a scoresheet). The number of the entering player is on the left of the slash mark; the number of the player being replaced is on the right of the slash mark.

During a dead ball in which the substitution request occurs, immediately notify the umpire if a substitute is entering or attempting to enter the game and is not listed on the roster. This, of course, would be an illegal entry. Don't count an illegal substitution as an entry against the team. Also notify the umpire if a substitute does any of the following:

- Reenters or attempts to reenter the game
- Attempts to reenter as a second substitute during a single time-out period
- Is the team's 19th substitution
- Assumes a position out of the serving order
- Attempts to reenter the game after being replaced by the exceptional substitution procedure
- Attempts to enter or reenter the game after having been disqualified

Communicating With the Umpire   In carrying out your duties as the scorer, you will find occasion to communicate with the umpire, as in the just-mentioned cases of illegal substitutions. Other times when you should communicate with the umpire—always during a dead ball—include when a team requests an illegal time-out, when there is a disagreement about the score, or when there is an illegal replacement.

During each time-out, notify the umpire how many time-outs each team has used.

Also point to the number "24" (or "14") and notify the umpire when a team reaches game point, preferably immediately following the end of the rally that puts a team at game point. You can do this verbally or through a predetermined signal you've set up with the umpire. You should also let the umpire know when a previous violation (for illegal equipment, time-out, uniform or unsporting conduct) has been recorded for the same individual. For subsequent violations of uniform or equipment by the same team during the match, award a point or loss of rally to the opponent. Unsporting behavior falls under the card penalties.

Throughout the match, be prepared to answer the umpire's questions regarding the number of substitutions a team has made and the number of time-outs it has taken.

Timer

The timer sits at the officials' table next to the scorer and aids the scorer. If you are the timer, you should report to the referee no less than 20 minutes before the match is to begin. Inspect the timing device, testing it to make sure it works. You should have a stopwatch available as a backup in case the timing device malfunctions.

If the timing and scoring devices are contained in a single unit, you are responsible for operating the unit. If a horn or other sound device is available to notify officials of the ends of time-outs, you operate this device as well.

Either the referee or the umpire will direct you to start the clock for the prematch warm-ups, which are timed on the scoreboard clock. If the umpire requests you to do so, sound the horn at the end of each portion of the timed warm-up. Most umpires, however, signal each segment of the timed warm-up with a whistle blast.

During the match, your timing responsibilities fall into three areas: timing the intermission between games, timing time-outs and using an audio signal to notify on-court officials of an improper serve or other problem that requires their attention. Following is guidance in all three areas.

- *Intermissions.* Start the clock for the three-minute intermission between games upon the referee's whistle directing teams to their respective team benches. Give an audio signal after 2:45 of the intermission has expired, and again at the end of the three minutes (unless both teams are already on the court).

- *Time-outs.* Time the interval for each time-out beginning with the official's signal, and give an audio signal (as a warning) at the end of 45 seconds and, if necessary, at the end of the entire 60 seconds. For an injury time-out, begin the interval with the official's signal and give an audio signal at 30 seconds unless play has resumed or the official indicates that a decision regarding the injured player's status has been made.

- *Audio signals.* Give an audio signal when the scorer indicates that the wrong player has served the ball. Give this signal when the server contacts the ball. Also give an audio signal for any other problem that the umpire or referee needs to address. Sound your horn only when the ball is dead. Never give an audio signal during play or after the referee has given the signal for the serve (except for improper server or illegal replacement on contact of the ball).

Line Judge

The final official in a volleyball game, the line judge, has a high-profile role because he or she determines whether hits are out or in. The line judge makes the initial call of in bounds or out of bounds; however, that call can be overruled by the referee, if deemed incorrect. Before you learn about the line judge's responsibilities, let's take a moment to consider selection and training.

Good line judges are essential for a volleyball match. Nothing is more frustrating to a team or a coach than an incorrect line call that goes against them. Understandably, line judges are human and are going to make mistakes, but with proper instruction, training, and experience, those mistakes should be minimal.

It is the host school's responsibility to select, instruct and train line judges. Long before the season begins, school personnel should recruit and select judges—preferably adults. Paying judges will not make them perform better, but proper instruction and training will. Schools that "train" line judges right before a match are asking for trouble. This time should be reserved for a brief, general review of their positioning and duties, as described in the next sections.

Positioning

If you are a line judge, you should report to the referee at least 20 minutes before the start of the match. The referee will review your responsibilities and assign you and the other judge or judges to your positions. You should hold your position throughout the match, although that doesn't mean you don't move.

In general, you will be at the intersection of the left sideline and the end line, and you should move as necessary to be in the best position for an unobstructed, straight-on view of the end line or sideline so you can make the proper call (see figure 2.4). You should be close enough to the intersection to have a straight sight line of either line with just a slight shift of your body.

You might also need to move to get out of the way of the server. When a ball is going toward the sideline on the other side of the net, you should move, if necessary, to be lined up with that sideline (see figure 2.5). Make sure, however, that you never enter the playing area, and be alert to avoid being struck by the ball or interfering with a player's opportunity to make a play.

As a line judge you should position yourself in certain areas during time-outs and between games. During time-outs, stand at the intersection of the attack line and the sideline, on your side of the court, nearest the referee. The line judge on the serving team's side holds the game ball during time-outs. Between games, report to a designated neutral area, such as at or behind the officials' table.

FIGURE 2.4   Line judge positioning.

FIGURE 2.5   Line judge positioning for a ball on the sideline.

Duties and Responsibilities

Your main responsibility as a line judge is to determine whether balls on or near the sideline and end line nearest to you are in or out. If any part of the ball touches any part of the boundary line, the ball is in bounds.

Line judge hand signals are shown in figures 2.6a through 2.6f. The line judge's use of flags is optional (see figures 2.7a through 2.7e on page 28 for flag signals).

In addition, you are to indicate when a player touches a ball that is going out of bounds on the player's side of the net (see figure 2.6d). Use the out-of-bounds signal, as shown in figure 2.6c, to indicate when the ball touches the ceiling or an overhead obstruction following a team's third contact or as the ball crosses the net toward the opponent's court (this is most important if the touch is out of view of, or not noticed by, the umpire or referee) or when there is a net violation (i.e., when the ball does not cross the net entirely between the net antennas or antennas extended). Line judges should also indicate when a server commits a line violation, using the line violation signal as shown in figure 2.6e.

Whether you use your hands or flags, make your decision quickly and decisively, without regard to the call being made by the line judge on the other side of the court. Hold your signal until you're sure the referee has seen it. Note that on some hard-hit balls deep in a corner, both judges might be calling the ball—one for the sideline and one for the end line. In such cases, one line judge may signal the ball in and the other may signal it out. If either judge signals out, the call is out. Otherwise, only the line judge who has the line involved in the call should signal.

Special Situations

Line judges need to be aware of a few special situations that involve serving.

First, if you are the serving team line judge, make sure you're in good position to watch for line violations even as you avoid interfering with a server who serves near the left sideline. Be ready to observe the sidelines and net antennas the moment the server contacts the ball. After contact, quickly resume your original position.

Second, if the server serves from the left third of the service area, you should move directly back and in line with the extension of the left sideline, out of the peripheral view of the server, until the server contacts the ball. Then quickly move back into position at the intersection of the end line and left sideline.

Third, if you are the receiving team line judge, position yourself in line with the sideline for which you are responsible so you can observe the sideline and net antennas as the ball crosses the net.

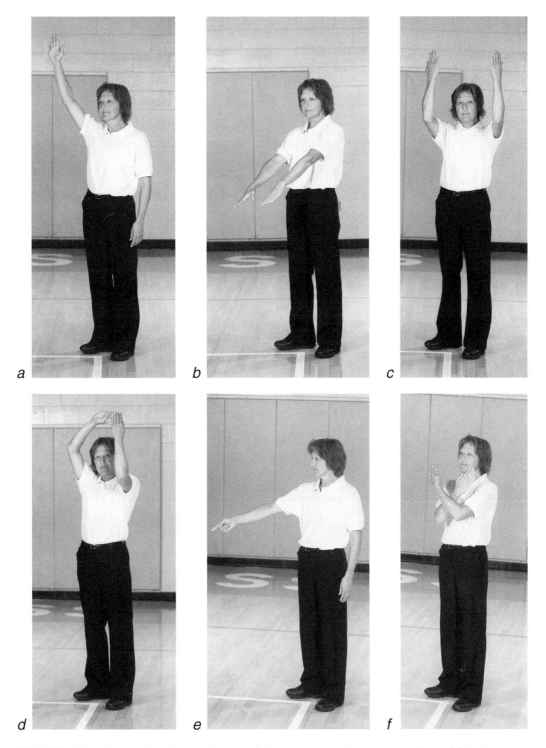

FIGURE 2.6   Line judge hand signals: *(a)* obtaining referee's attention; *(b)* in bounds; *(c)* out of bounds or antenna violation; *(d)* ball touched; *(e)* line violation; *(f)* view of play blocked.

FIGURE 2.7 Line judge flag signals: *(a)* ball in; *(b)* impossible to judge; *(c)* ball out after contact with a player; *(d)* ball outside or touching the antenna; *(e)* obtain referee's attention or ball out.

Characteristics of a Good Line Judge

At the high school level, line judges are often students or volunteers and are not certified volleyball officials. To help maintain professionalism in the sport, line judges should follow these guidelines:

- Know the rules, your responsibilities and areas of coverage, your positioning and how to communicate your calls. Be willing to undertake the proper instruction and training to learn these things.
- Arrive at the match, appropriately dressed, at least 20 minutes before the match begins, and report promptly to the referee for instructions and a prematch meeting with other officials.
- Be courteous to other line judges, officials, coaches and players. Perform your duties in a confident, quiet, efficient manner. Show respect for the calls of other line judges. Show respect for and accept, without question, all decisions by the referee. Respond positively to suggestions and directions from the referee.
- Remain aloof from players and spectators during the match. Ignore spectator criticism; maintain complete concentration on the game.
- Make objective, quick and decisive calls using the correct signals. Be alert and ready to move quickly into the best position to make a call without interfering with play.
- Be neutral in terms of the action. Don't react negatively or positively to plays or calls; simply maintain your proper position and make your calls.

That covers the essential duties of the referee, umpire, scorer, assistant scorer, timer and line judges. In the next chapter we cover the specific prematch, match and postmatch responsibilities and procedures of the referee and umpire.

PART II

VOLLEYBALL
OFFICIATING MECHANICS

CHAPTER 3

MATCH PROCEDURES

In the last chapter you learned about the essential duties of all the officials—the referee, umpire, scorer, assistant scorer, timer and line judges. In this chapter you'll explore, in detail, the match procedures and responsibilities undertaken by the referee and the umpire before, during and after the match. Along the way you'll learn about preventive officiating techniques, substitution procedures, tracking back-row players, using your whistle, signaling, communicating with coaches and many other critical issues.

Prematch Procedures and Responsibilities

The referee and the umpire have many responsibilities before a match begins. In the role of either official, you should arrive at the court, in uniform, at least 30 minutes before the scheduled starting time and begin immediately to tend to your prematch duties.

When you get to the site of the match, report to the host management, who should assign you and your fellow official a room or rooms where you can change into your uniforms, if necessary, and confer with each other. Find out where management personnel will be during the match, and discuss with them the procedures for removing an unruly spectator and for handling other problems or emergencies. Also discuss any special prematch ceremonies of which you need to be aware, such as Parents' Night introductions, standard team introductions and the playing of the national anthem.

Before the day of the match, you and the other official should talk briefly to determine who will be the umpire and who will be the referee. There's no set procedure here; it's up to you two to decide. Sometimes the more experienced official will be the referee, but it's not necessarily decided according to seniority.

Before you go onto the court, you and the other official should introduce yourselves to each other and discuss umpire and referee coverage.

Informal Officiating Signals

In addition to the formal signals used when officiating volleyball (see the appendix on page 115 for examples of these signals), you can also use informal hand signals to communicate with your fellow official on the court. You will want to discuss informal signals you want to use with the umpire or referee you are officiating with and make sure you're clear on the signals before you take to the court. Figure 3.1 shows some examples of informal signals.

a

b

c

d

e

FIGURE 3.1   Informal offIciating signals: *(a)* game or match point; *(b)* four hits; *(c)* back-row player violation; *(d)* position of setter prior to serve; *(e)* illegal hit.

Some of the situations you should discuss include those involving net play, center-line fouls, touches on blocks, ball handling, serve reception, ground rules and any informal hand signals you'll use to communicate with each other during the match (see "Informal Officiating Signals," for more information). You might also want to talk about patterns of serve reception, unusual plays or anything distinctive about the teams involved.

Once on the court, the referee is responsible for checking it and the game equipment with the umpire (as discussed in detail in "Inspecting Game Equipment" on the following page), and then for informing both coaches of any equipment that does not meet rules specifications. The host management is responsible for providing legal equipment and making sure the facility is properly prepared for the match. The referee must meet with the line judges to assign them to their positions, go over signaling duties, review the service area, inform them where they are to stand during time-outs and show them the designated neutral area where they can be seated between games. If there is a ball-return system, the referee should meet with the people involved to review the process for retrieval and delivery of the ball to the next server.

If you are the umpire, in addition to other duties outlined prior to this, you should make sure the timer, scorer and assistant scorer are located opposite the referee and see that a scoreboard is visible to teams and spectators and that the timer is assigned to operate it. Meet with the scorer, assistant scorer and timer to review their duties (including identifying each team's first server and placing that number as the first player's number on the scoresheet). Answer any questions they have, and discuss with the scorer how you will communicate substitutions and unsporting conduct violations. Remind the scorer to record, in the comments section of the scoresheet, situations involving uniform and equipment violations, unconscious players and yellow and red cards. Remind the assistant scorer to record all substitutions as well as libero replacements.

Prematch Conference

The referee, aided by the umpire, conducts a prematch conference with a captain and coach from each team. The referee and umpire should be positioned in front of the officials' table facing the court when conducting this meeting. The captains and coaches will be to the side of the referee and umpire on their appropriate sides of the center line extended. The conference should be brief and businesslike, but pleasant. Examples of items covered in such a conference are as follows (conference items might differ depending on the situation):

1. Introduce captains, coaches and officials to each other, and verify that the home team has selected its bench.

Before each match, the referee and umpire are required to meet with the home management to discuss local ground rules in accordance with the written rules. Because no two gymnasiums are alike, there are rulings—called ground rules—that must be made according to the configuration of the court and the surrounding area. Using the *NFHS Rules Book* as a guide, make rulings to address any irregularities in the facility. Examples of ground rules are nonplayable areas, vertical backboards, adjacent courts and other objects considered out of bounds. In discussing these elements, you will want to clarify the following:

- *Court boundaries and markings.* Are all the boundary lines there? Are they wide enough? Do the lines contrast in color to the floor? Is the center line continuous across the entire width of the court? Is it a 2-inch solid or bordered line? If the center line is not continuous, request that host management provide a temporary 2-inch center line.

- *Net equipment and padding.* Are the net antennas attached in line with the outside edge of the sideline and properly secured? Are the standards, referee platform, and cables properly padded? Is the tensioning device covered? If the equipment is not properly padded or covered and cannot be corrected, you should not allow the match to be conducted, and you should notify the state association.

- *Net height.* Check the net for proper height by measuring it at the center and each end. Test net tension by throwing a ball into the middle of the net at a moderate speed from about 5 feet away. The bottom of the net should not move into the plane of the other court. The ball should rebound slightly and should not drop straight down or become lodged in the net. Check the net a second time after the warm-up.

- *Game balls.* Inspect each game ball to see that it is spherical with a molded cover of white genuine or simulated leather, is properly inflated and meets all other rules specifications. If you are the referee, you have the final decision on game balls. Be sure to carry an accurate pressure measuring device to help you in your decisions.

- *Team benches.* The umpire should make sure the team benches, starting at the 10-foot line opposite the referee, are at least 6 feet from the court boundaries (10 feet is preferred) and outside the out-of-bounds extension of the center line. When bleachers are used for the team benches, a tape mark should be used to designate the end of the bench closest to the net.

- *Referee platform.* The referee should check the platform for proper height and stability. Is the platform high enough to see play above the net? If not, ask the home management to increase its height.

2. Explain local ground rules, such as nonplayable areas, vertical backboards, and so on.

3. Review rules regarding player equipment and uniforms, including hair devices, hair adornment and jewelry. Ask coaches to verify that all their players are wearing legal uniforms and equipment.

4. Discuss your expectations for good sporting behavior.

5. Explain the procedure that will be used for ball retrieval.

6. Remind coaches and captains that only the floor captain can request a time-out from the playing court or ask what call was made. Also remind them that no one, including captains or coaches, can question judgment calls.

7. Remind captains and coaches that players should play until they hear a whistle. When appropriate, players should return the ball promptly by rolling it under the net.

8. Review the protocol for greeting the opponent, starting a game, ending a game, changing courts and participating in the coin toss before the deciding game.

9. Conduct the coin toss for the initial game (see "Coin Toss" for more information).

10. Ask if anyone has any questions. Once questions are answered, wish both captains and coaches a good match, and remind them to share information from this conference with their teams before the match begins.

Coin Toss

The referee will conduct the coin toss to conclude the prematch conference, just prior to the prescribed timed warm-ups, at least 15 minutes before the first game. As mentioned, a captain and coach from each team are present for this conference and coin toss. Before tossing the coin, instruct the visiting team captain to call heads or tails while the coin is in the air. Then toss the coin and catch it (if you drop it, toss it again). After catching the coin, do not turn it over; just show it to the players and coaches.

The winner of the toss chooses to serve or receive. The referee reports the results of the toss to the scorer, and the umpire instructs the timer when to start the clock for the prescribed timed warm-up (see the following section for more information on the warm-up procedure).

Another coin toss takes place prior to the deciding game, which is the fifth game in a best-of-five match or the third game in a best-of-three match (see "The Deciding Game Coin Toss" on page 56 for more information about this coin toss). The home team captain calls this toss. The winner of the toss chooses one of the following: to serve or to receive, or to occupy a certain court. The loser of the toss gets the remaining choice.

Warm-Up

Once the prematch conference has taken place and the coin toss has been made, the warm-up period begins. Typically, the warm-up is 20 minutes in duration and is conducted based on state association or conference determinations.

If the warm-up does not need to be run according to state or conference recommendations, or a situation arises in which the length of warm-up and how it is to be conducted must be altered, this may be done by mutual agreement of the coaches.

During the warm-up time, the umpire obtains the rosters and lineups from the coaches and delivers them to the scorer. Ultimately, the coaches are responsible for delivering the lineups, but it is also good preventive officiating for the umpire to approach a coach if the deadline is nearing and the coach hasn't turned in the lineup yet. The scorer as well as the assistant scorer should write these lineups, in the serving order given, on the scoresheet and tracking sheet. The umpire will check the official scoresheet for the proper listing of serving order and will check the libero tracking sheet. Another preventive act by the umpire is to make certain the coach is not intending to use the libero player for that game if one is not listed on the lineup.

As the teams warm up, all officials should watch them to prepare mentally for the match. Watch how they handle the ball, and become familiar with who the setters and hitters are and the attack patterns they use. Don't talk so that you can be overheard or use gestures that might be misunderstood by players, coaches or spectators. Take this time to practice some preventive officiating to minimize having to begin the match with a penalty, such as taking time to check each team's roster against the players on the court when their numbers are visible. If warm-up jackets cover the uniform numbers, count the number of players on the floor and compare it to the number of players on the roster. Also check for jewelry; players are not allowed to wear jewelry, even in warm-ups. If you observe a player wearing jewelry during the warm-up, call this to the coach's attention so the player can remove the jewelry. For other preventive measures, see "Preventive Officiating" later in this chapter.

Beginning the Match

After the warm-up, the national anthem, the introduction of teams and officials and any other prematch ceremonies, the procedures for officials are as follows (although in writing this appears to be a long procedure, it generally happens quickly and efficiently):

- The referee takes a position on the referee platform, and the umpire and line judges move into position.
- Once all officials are in position, the referee blows the whistle to direct the starting players to their respective end lines.
- The referee blows a second whistle and signals the players onto the playing court. If the teams have indicated during the prematch conference that they want to shake hands prior to the match, this should be done at the net when the teams report onto the court.
- The umpire uses the lineup card (not the scoresheet) to verify that the players are in their proper positions. If a libero player is waiting on the sideline to enter as a replacement, the umpire authorizes this player to do so once the lineups are checked.
- Prior to the serve, the umpire identifies the back-row players on both teams.
- When the umpire has ensured that the lineups are correct, the umpire rolls the ball to the first server and assumes the proper position on the receiving team's side of the court.

Proper Signaling Technique

Signaling is the essential way you communicate your calls, decisions and other matters of importance to players, coaches and fans. Therefore, it's critical that you know when, how and what to signal, and that you do so in a way that's clear for all to understand. Your ability to signal will indicate to others your competence as an official and will help you maintain control of the match.

Remember to use this separate and sequential procedure each time you signal:

1. Blow your whistle quickly and with authority.
2. Signal the violation, holding your hand and arm signals on the side of the offending team. Your arm should be held high enough and the signal should be held long enough for everyone to see.
3. Signal replay or indicate team that is serving next.
4. Verbalize the decision when necessary. (For example, a play at the net might need verbal clarification if it's not apparent whether the defense's net violation occurred before or after the offense's illegal contact.)

The best officials know not only how to respond in any situation during a contest, but also how to prevent certain situations from happening. Here are some ways you can use preventive officiating to minimize distractions, delays and penalties:

Before the Match

- Check each team's roster against the players on the court. Count players on the court and compare that with the number of players on the team roster submitted by the coaches.

- Check players for illegal equipment and jewelry and for open wounds, bleeding or excessive blood on the uniform. Check the legality of all protective devices when requested by a coach.

- Discuss your expectations of sporting behavior with coaches and team captains during the prematch conference.

- Verify with each coach the legality of players' uniforms and equipment. Remind coaches of their responsibility for accurate rosters and lineups. Make sure each coach has a designated floor captain listed on the lineup. If the libero is the captain, have the coach identify who the captain will be when the libero is not in the game.

- Prior to each game, the umpire checks the lineup for each team. Make corrections so the players and the serving order correspond with the written lineup when the game begins. If no libero player is listed on the lineup, you may wish to ask the coaches to be certain they do not plan to use the libero.

During the Match

- Ask a coach who the captain is when the current floor captain is removed through a substitution.

- Warn the serving team of a possible screening situation.

- Inform coaches when their teams request their 15th, 16th, 17th and 18th substitutions.

- Ignore a substitution or time-out request after the referee has signaled for the serve.

- Deny a request for a second substitution during the same time-out or dead ball.

- Correct, without penalty, an improper substitution procedure if it does not delay the game.

- Correct any illegal libero replacements without penalty unless it delays the game.

- Making sure the line judges are in their places, the referee establishes eye contact with the umpire to receive an indication of readiness from her or him. If possible, the referee should do the same with the teams' floor captains. The referee then scans the court, beginning with the receiving team, then going to the bench area, the scorer and umpire, the serving team and finally the server. After identifying the back-row players on both teams and being assured that everyone is ready, the referee blows the whistle and gives the signal for serve.

Match Procedures

Although you have plenty of prematch responsibilities, your duties and obligations don't end there, as you well know. In this section you'll learn the procedures that will help you effectively fulfill your duties during a match, including specific referee and umpire responsibilities and both formal and informal signals that you'll use to communicate throughout the match.

Common Responsibilities

During a match, some responsibilities are shared by the referee and the umpire, who must work as a team to keep the match running smoothly. The referee and umpire must continually help each other watch for things such as possible back-row attacks or illegal ball handling. They also should develop and use discreet informal signals (see "Informal Officiating Signals" on page 34). Following are some specific responsibilities that both the referee and umpire share during a match:

- Prior to the match, officials use the starting lineups to help them determine the setters' starting positions. Once the teams take the court for lineup verification, the umpire can assist the referee by discreetly advising him or her on the setters' positions.

- Before every live ball, both officials should make a mental note of where each team's setter is positioned. If you are the referee, check the receiving team for readiness and note whether its setter is in the front or back row. Then check the serving team for readiness and note the setter's positions prior to the whistle and signal for serve. If you are the umpire, look through the net to spot the serving team's setter and then check the receiving team's lineup prior to contact of the serve. Both officials should repeat this practice prior to each serve throughout the match.

- The referee and umpire should track back-row players and watch for illegal alignments at the contact of the serve, for back-row attacks

Using Your Whistle

Your whistle is one primary way you communicate on the court. Whether you are the referee or the umpire, you should have a whistle on a lanyard and carry a spare whistle in your officiating bag. Here are a few pointers about when and how to use your whistle:

- Keep the whistle in your mouth during play and drop it from your mouth when speaking. When you sound your whistle, do so loudly, firmly and decisively. Adjust your whistle loudness to the surroundings, using a louder whistle in a crowded, noisy gym. Also, blow it only long enough for it to be effective.
- Play begins and ends with an official's whistle. When a rally is finished, the play is blown dead immediately by either the referee's or umpire's whistle.
- There's no need to repeat your fellow official's whistle when the ball is blown dead. The umpire *does*, however, mirror the visual signal for violations, points and replays or re-serves. The referee also mirrors the signals initiated by the umpire's whistle.
- The umpire's whistle should be different from the referee's whistle; this helps people know where the whistle came from. One suggestion is for the umpire to use a short, double whistle and for the referee to use a single, slightly longer whistle (except for stoppage of play, when both should use a single short whistle.
- Should both teams end the time-out before 60 seconds expire, the umpire blows the whistle to signal the number of time-outs each team has taken. (If the umpire is still checking the scoresheet, the referee blows the whistle.)

and for blocks from the back row. The two officials should discuss before a match how they want to watch for these back-row issues and communicate any illegal situations.

- Both officials should be aware of how many setters each team uses and what type of offense the teams are running. If a team runs a 4-2 offense, for example, setters will rarely use back-row attacks. In a 6-2 offense, on the other hand, the potential for a back-row attack is greater. The setter might be coming from the back row on every rotation. A team running a 5-1 offense makes tracking the setter a bit more difficult. Whatever the situation, the referee and the umpire should be alert on every rotation.

Referee Responsibilities

As referee, you remain on the platform throughout each game, except possibly during an official's time-out and for the coin toss prior to the deciding game. (It's preferable to remain on the platform throughout the game; your leaving it might be interpreted to mean that the umpire doesn't know how to do his or her job.) You are responsible for seeing that a whistle is blown and visual signals are given for all dead balls, violations, penalties, time-outs, substitutions and serves. At times it might be necessary also to verbalize a call; for example, when you call illegal alignment on a team, you can indicate which players are overlapped, or when you administer a card for a conduct violation, you can verbally indicate who is receiving the violation and why.

You have numerous other responsibilities during a match. In this section we'll explore those responsibilities, including your supervisory control; your responsibilities before, during and after the serve; administering cards; how to go about your duties at the ends of games and matches; and other duties as well.

The better you are able to fulfill these duties, the smoother a match will go. Learn them here and put them into practice as you continue to hone your abilities through experience.

Supervisory Control Your authority begins when you arrive onsite and continues until you verify the final score of the match and initial the scoresheet. This authority extends over the teams and the other officials. Part of this control is manifested in your authority to make the final decision concerning matters not specifically covered by the rules or when there's a conflict in a call between officials. You can and should correct a confirmed error by another official, and cancel points if appropriate, provided you make the correction prior to the contact of the first serve following a loss of rally. In addition, you may also replace a scorer (or assistant scorer, if applicable), timer or line judge who is not performing his or her duties properly.

Your authority also extends beyond the court. If you determine that crowd behavior is negatively affecting play, you should temporarily suspend play and direct host management to address the problem. If no administrator is present, the responsibility for resolving the situation lies with the host head coach. If the situation is not or cannot be resolved in a reasonable amount of time, you should suspend the match. The state association will determine whether the match is resumed from the point of suspension or declared a forfeit.

The Serve Before giving the signal for serve, do a visual sweep to see whether all players, coaches and officials are ready. Establish eye contact with the umpire to make sure that she or he is ready. Remember that any requests for time-outs, substitutions or serving order checks must be made during a dead ball.

After you signal for the serve, as shown in figures 3.2*a* and 3.2*b*, start a discreet five-second count. At the contact of the serve, watch the serving team for possible illegal alignment at the moment of contact of serve as well as potential screening by the server's teammates if the served ball passes directly over the player(s) (see chapter 5 for more information). Once the ball has been legally served, watch the flight of the ball to see that it legally crosses the net.

If the server releases the ball for service, then catches it or drops it to the floor, signal for a re-serve (see figure 3.3). This cancels the first serve attempt and gives the server a second and final attempt to serve.

When a team is playing with fewer than six players because of illness, injury or disqualification, you should signal a loss of rally and awarding of point by extending the arm with the palm perpendicular to the floor toward the opponent when, upon rotating to serve, the vacant position is the right-back position (see figure 3.4).

Ball Handling   During play, follow the ball and concentrate on ball handling. As the play progresses, constant activity—passes, sets, spikes and blocks—changes the flight of the ball and player positions. Therefore, you must constantly observe and evaluate each situation as it takes place. Watch for illegal hits and blocks, back-row player fouls and net fouls.

In evaluating ball handling, look ahead of the ball and focus on the part of the receiving player's body that will contact the ball. When the ball is in play near the net, concentrate on the top of the net downward. Continue to follow, or anticipate, the flight of the ball when it leaves the net area. When the ball hits the floor near any line, whistle the ball dead; then look at the line judge responsible for that line before giving a signal.

Time-Outs   If both teams are ready to play prior to the 60 seconds expiring, and the umpire is still checking the scoresheet, blow your whistle to signal the end of the time-out. Following a team time-out, the umpire whistles and signals how many time-outs each team has used. As referee, you should blow your whistle only when the umpire is busy with another responsibility, but you should always mirror the umpire's signal, indicating the same number of time-outs.

Cards   You are responsible for administering cards for unsporting conduct violations and assessing penalties when specified. Never let unsporting conduct occur without penalizing it. If there are multiple offenders, make sure each offender is penalized.

If you are initiating the warning or disqualification, tell the umpire the number of the player(s) or which coach is receiving the card(s). Make

FIGURE 3.2 Referee signaling for the serve.

FIGURE 3.3 Referee signaling for a re-serve.

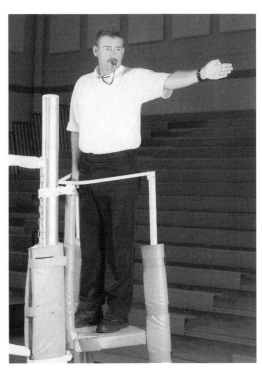

FIGURE 3.4 Referee signaling loss of rally and awarding of point.

FIGURE 3.5   Referee issuing a card.

sure the umpire has also identified the offenders and verified that the scorer has recorded the information on the scoresheet. If a player is disqualified, you must notify, or request the umpire to notify, the appropriate coach regarding the reason for the disqualification. When the umpire sees or hears an action or response that necessitates a card, he or she communicates this to you by moving to the offending team's side of the net and taking a few steps onto the court toward you. The umpire holds the card(s) in the middle of his or her chest and indicates verbally the number of the offending player(s) or coach. It is then your responsibility to administer the card or cards.

To administer a card, hold it in your hand on the offending team's side of the court with your arm outstretched, your elbow bent at 90 degrees and your hand held head-high (see figure 3.5). When administering the red and yellow cards together, such as in a disqualification as described later, duplicate this process, holding one card in each hand.

There are different types of violations, depending on the severity of the offense or the number of times an offense has occurred. When a card is issued it shall be recorded on the scoresheet, and it is also suggested that it be recorded on the umpire's lineup card. Here is a breakdown of the violations that warrant cards:

- *Warning.* For a first minor offense, you administer a yellow card at the first dead ball. The warning is recorded in the comments section on the scoresheet and on the umpire's lineup card. No penalty is assessed.

- *Penalty.* For a second minor offense by the same person, or for a single serious offense, you administer a red card at the first dead ball. A point is awarded the opponent, and the penalty is recorded in the comments section on the scoresheet and on the umpire's lineup card.

- *Disqualification.* For a third minor or second serious offense by the same person, or a single flagrant offense, display the yellow and red cards apart (usually at the first dead ball). The offender is disqualified from further participation in the match and may be removed from the vicinity of the team bench provided there are authorized school personnel available to supervise. (When the offender is a coach or other adult team personnel, the offender will be removed from the premises.) A point is awarded to the opponent, and you or the umpire should notify the appropriate coach of the reason for the disqualification. The disqualification is recorded in the comments section of the scoresheet.

- *Forfeit.* If a disqualified person violates the conduct rule following disqualification, the offender's team forfeits the match. Also, if the coach is removed from the premises and no other authorized school personnel are available, the team forfeits the match. Finally, unless state association rules determine otherwise, if a team refuses to play when you have directed them to do so, the team forfeits the match.

In addition, here are a few miscellaneous points about issuing cards:

- All cards carry over from game to game throughout the match; the umpire may keep notations on the lineup card. The scorer notifies the umpire of any previous violations by the same person.
- When unsporting conduct occurs from the bench or the court, and the officials cannot determine the specific offender(s), issue the warning or penalty to the coach.
- Any cards issued for unsporting conduct prior to the first game or between games should be administered at the beginning of the game immediately following the violation. After lineups are recorded, the card is recorded in the comments section on the scoresheet for the game in which it is administered.
- Do not recognize requests for time-outs, serving order checks, substitutions, and so on, until you have administered the card.
- If the team captain asks in a proper manner, you should give the reason for the penalty without discussing it further.

Ends of Games and Matches When it appears a team has won a game, blow your whistle and give the end-of-game signal (see figure 3.6) directing the players to their respective end lines. After visually confirming the score with the umpire, blow your whistle and direct the teams to their appropriate team bench areas.

After the nondeciding game that is just prior to the deciding game (the fifth game in a best-of-five match or the third game in a best-of-three), the teams remain on the end line while you call the captains to the center of the court near the referee platform for the coin toss. You conduct the toss (unless you ask the umpire to do so), instructing the home team captain

FIGURE 3.6   Referee signaling end of game.

to call the toss. Following the coin toss, blow your whistle and signal the teams to change courts and team benches or to return to the same team benches, depending on the result of the toss.

Following other nondeciding games, after you have confirmed the score of the game, blow your whistle and signal the teams to change courts and team benches. The players on the court move counterclockwise along the sideline and past the standards to their new team benches. Players on the benches simply switch.

At the end of the match, blow your whistle and give the end-of-game signal directing the players to their respective end lines. Visually confirm the score with the umpire; then blow your whistle and direct the players to their respective team benches. The teams decide whether they wish to shake hands with their opponents. Then verify the score of the match by initialing the scoresheet. Once you initial the scoresheet, no change can be made to the score.

Umpire Responsibilities

As the umpire, you also have a wide range of duties, including duties related to beginning a game and serving; keeping the lineup card; covering the play and making calls; and communicating with coaches regarding substitutions, time-outs and other matters. In the rest of this section you'll learn how to handle these responsibilities.

The Serve   Prior to each signal for serve, you should make eye contact with the referee to let the referee know you are ready for the serve to take place.

During the serve, stand outside the sideline, back from the standard and square to the court on the receiving team's side (see figure 3.7). Although you want to maintain a position that gives you a clear view of the ball, you must not interfere with any player's legitimate effort to play the ball.

Watch the receiving team for possible illegal alignment as you listen for the contact of the serve. For example, a setter may move before the ball is served. You have to watch the setter to ascertain whether the movement results in illegal alignment—that is, if the back-row setter has at least part of one foot in contact with the floor closer to the center line than a foot of the corresponding front-row player at contact of serve (see chapter 5 for more information). If you determine that no overlapping occurred, move quickly to the defensive side of the net.

Lineup Card   A lineup card, as shown in figure 3.8, is a valuable tool that helps you carry out your duties as umpire. This card shall be used to check the position of players on the court prior to the beginning of each game. Keep the lineup card and a

FIGURE 3.7   Proper umpire positioning for a serve.

Centerville   Red

2 1 2 1

4c

   6

8 3 8 3

10 5

12

T.O. 1/2

1̸ 2̸ 3̸ 4̸ 5̸ 6̸ 7̸ 8 9 10 11 12 13 14 15 16 17 18

FIGURE 3.8   Sample lineup card.

pencil or marker with you during the game. You may record the following information on the lineup card:

- *Serving order.* This is a valuable tool to help you, at a glance, tell whether the players are in the correct alignment at contact of the serve.

- *Substitutions.* With the information on your card, you can immediately recognize illegal substitutions. Without a lineup card, it's difficult to keep track of overlapping when there have been many substitutions.

- *Time-outs.* It is your job to notify the referee of how many time-outs each team has used. At the end of the time-out and just prior to the serve, the referee and you signal how many time-outs each team has used. Keep track of the time-outs at the bottom of the card.

- *Captain.* Place a C beside the team captain's number in the serving order. This is important for you to know because only the captain can confer with officials.

- *Player identification.* Place a circle around a player's number to designate a certain player (e.g., a setter who comes from the back row, or a back-row hitter).

- *Yellow and red cards.* Record all cards issued.

Coverage and Calls   Your primary responsibility is the net area. However, if there is no activity at the net, you can broaden your field of vision to assist the referee in other areas of the court.

During net play, focus on the center line and net area from the floor up. Watch the center line, move your eyes up to the net, be alert for touches on the block and move down the net and back to the center line. Resist the temptation to follow the ball away from the net during net play. You should position yourself on the blocking side of the net at an angle that allows a clear view through the entire length of the net to see touches of the ball, net fouls, back-row player fouls and center line violations by both the attacking and defending teams. You should continually transition back and forth to each side of the net when hits are made by using a technique such as taking a step behind the body, as shown in figure 3.9. To maintain the best visibility of the court, you must make this transition quickly.

The referee depends on the umpire to watch for center-line and net violations while he or she follows the flight of the ball and observes ball handling. You will assist with ball-handling violations only when these violations are clearly out of the referee's view, such as when a player has his or her back to the referee or plays a ball near the floor. You will initiate a call by blowing your whistle, moving to the offending team's side of the net and then signaling the violation.

When the call involves a net violation or a player across the center line, indicate the number of the offending player to the referee who, in turn, signals the number to the bench. On calls by the referee, step away from the standards and repeat the referee's signal, but don't repeat the referee's whistle.

When you see an action or hear a remark that you deem to be an unsporting conduct violation, move to the offending team's side of the net and take a few steps onto the court toward the referee. Hold the appropriate card or cards in the middle of your chest and indicate verbally to the referee the offending coach or the number of the offending player or players (see figure 3.10). The referee will then administer the card, and you should move to the officials' table to confirm the violation with the scorer and make certain that the warning, penalty or disqualification is recorded in the comments section of the scoresheet. In addition, if so requested by the referee, you should notify the appropriate coach of the reason for the disqualification.

FIGURE 3.9 Umpire transitioning to the other side of the net.

Finally, during dead balls, and especially after time-outs and intermissions, scan the playable area for new obstacles, encroaching fans and other safety hazards near the court before signaling readiness to the referee.

Substitutions After each point, glance toward each bench to see whether either coach is requesting a substitution. Look for an

FIGURE 3.10 Umpire issuing a card.

approaching substitute or a signal for a substitute from a coach. When you see a substitute or a signal for one, blow your whistle and signal for the substitute to enter. You are responsible for the expedient, efficient substitution of players. By requiring that proper procedures be followed and detecting illegal substitutions, you can prevent many problems.

Here are proper substitution procedures:

FIGURE 3.11   Coach signaling for a substitution.

1. The coach must visually signal a request for substitution, as shown in figure 3.11, or the substitute(s) must enter the substitution zone, which is near the sideline between the attack line extended and the center line extended, to constitute a request for substitution. If the coach stands to request a substitution, he or she may greet the replaced player and continue to stand in the libero replacement zone (between the attack line extended and the baseline extended) during any dead ball to instruct his or her players (however, the coach must be seated prior to the signal for next serve). If a card (yellow or red) is issued to the head coach, assistant coach(es) or team bench, the privilege is lost and the head coach must remain seated except to do any of the following:

- Request a time-out or substitution during a dead ball
- Ask the umpire to review the accuracy of the score, verify the number of time-outs used or verify the serving order of his or her team or proper server for the opponent
- Greet a replaced player
- Confer with players during a time-out
- Spontaneously react to an outstanding play
- Confer with officials during specifically requested time-outs
- Attend an injured player with permission from the official

2. To recognize the request for a substitution, you should whistle and signal for the substitution (see figure 3.12). The referee acknowledges this by repeating the signal.

3. While facing the court, you should immediately move near the scorer to facilitate the substitution as the substitute(s) and player(s) being replaced move to the sideline between the attack line and the center line facing each other, as shown in figure 3.13.

4. In a normal substitution situation, use the "authorization to enter" signal, as shown in figure 3.13, to release the substitutes to enter the court and the player(s) being replaced to return to the team bench, and then verify with the scorer that he or she has recorded the substitution(s).

5. Note the substitution on your lineup card (although it's not required, you may find it helpful). You and the scorer should check to make sure it is a legal substitute. On a team's 15th, 16th, 17th and 18th entries, notify the head coach.

6. The referee and you must make sure that substitutes take their proper positions on the court.

7. Return to your position on the side of the receiving team and indicate to the referee readiness for play to resume.

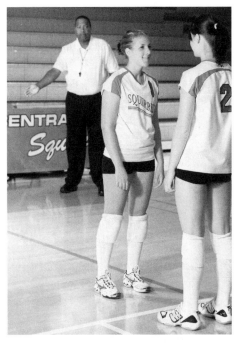

FIGURE 3.12 Umpire signaling for a substitution.

FIGURE 3.13 Umpire positioning during the substitution(s).

Time-Outs   Just as you should be on the lookout after each point for substitutions, also glance over toward each head coach after each play to see whether either is requesting a time-out. During a charged time-out, your duties are as follows:

1. Recognize the request with a double whistle and signal the time-out (see figures 3.14*a* and 3.14*b*).

2. Upon honoring the request for a time-out with a whistle and signal, report to the scorer which team has taken the time-out and remind the timer to start the clock. For example, you might say, "Time-out, Blue, please start the clock."

3. Make sure the game ball is held by the line judge standing at the intersection of the attack line and sideline on the side of the serving team.

4. Check with the scorer to make sure the time-out is recorded in the scoresheet for the appropriate team, and check the scoresheet for any individual score and team score discrepancies. Make sure the visible scoreboard agrees with the scoresheet.

5. Indicate the end of a charged time-out with a whistle followed by a signal to the referee of how many time-outs each team has used. The referee will then mirror the number of time-outs used by each

a   *b*

FIGURE 3.14   Umpire signaling a time-out.

team. You should release the match to the referee with an informal signal such as an extended arm with open hand toward the referee or by using eye contact.

6. End the time-out with a double whistle. (If both teams are on the court ready to play before 60 seconds have elapsed, blow your whistle to end the time-out.)

When an injury or illness occurs on the court, a team is not charged with a time-out. In this situation, an official's time-out is taken. Examples of when to call an official's time-out includes when a player is ill or injured, has an open wound, is bleeding or has excessive blood on the uniform. During any of these situations, either official should stop play at the earliest possible time and administer this interruption of play as an injury time-out. This is signaled using a time-out signal followed by a tap on top of the shoulders once with both hands. As umpire, you should make sure the clock is started after the time-out. Keep in mind that any injured or ill player must receive proper treatment before resuming participation.

During an official's time-out, remind the timer to start the clock for 30 seconds. The teams remain on the court. Before the 30 seconds expire, ask the coach for a decision regarding the player's status if one has not been made. If an injured player is to be replaced, play resumes only after the injured player can safely be moved. If there will be a long delay, allow the players to go to their benches or warm up a safe distance from the injured player.

When an official's time-out is called for an open wound, bleeding or excessive blood on the uniform, the player must receive proper treatment. If that can be accomplished within the 30 seconds or an additional charged time-out taken by the team (taken before the 30 seconds has ended in order to give the team 90 total seconds for the time-out), the player can remain in the game.

Scoresheet   During each time-out and at the end of the game, check the scoresheet to see that the individual and team scores for both teams are correct and correspond with the visible scoreboard. To prevent a delay at the end of each game, verify and signal game point just before a possible game point is served (see figure 3.15). After the referee has confirmed the game score using a signal, give the end-of-game signal (see figure 3.16) to the referee, initial the scoresheet, make sure the timer starts the three-minute clock when the referee blows the whistle to direct teams to their appropriate team benches and remind coaches to submit their lineups for the next game to the scorer not less than one minute prior to the end of the three-minute intermission.

FIGURE 3.15   Umpire signaling game point.

FIGURE 3.16   Umpire signaling end of game.

The Deciding Game Coin Toss   If so requested by the referee, you will conduct the coin toss prior to the deciding game. When this is the case, the referee will motion the captains from the end lines to the net to meet with you near the referee platform. Upon completion of the coin toss, send the captains back to their respective end lines; then signal to the referee for a change of court or for the teams to return to their respective benches. The referee will then blow his or her whistle and give the appropriate signal, using the same protocol as with the other end-of-game procedures. Verbalize to the referee who will serve first, and also report that to the scorer.

Postmatch Procedures

After the match, both the referee and umpire should complete their end-of-match responsibilities (checking and verifying the score and initialing the scoresheet) and then should leave the court together. As you do, neither avoid nor seek contact with coaches, but refrain from talking about any decisions with any spectators. Also make sure you don't make any public statements to the media or to anyone else about the match.

Continue to use exemplary conduct after leaving the court and while in the general geographic area (e.g., the school grounds and parking lot). Report promptly to the state association any irregularities or unsporting conduct in connection with the match.

That covers the prematch, match and postmatch procedures. Study them well! Your knowledge of the procedures surrounding a match, including your specific duties as referee or umpire, coupled with your knowledge of the rules and your ability to crisply execute signals, will go a long way toward helping you be a top-notch official.

CHAPTER 4

BALL-HANDLING VIOLATIONS

A back-row player passes the ball to the setter. As she attempts to set the ball, the ball slips off her hands a bit, but she manages to set the ball to a teammate. Is this legal, or is it a ball-handling violation?

Without seeing the play, of course, it's hard to judge. But in real life, with the play right in front of you, it can *still* be hard to judge. Yet you are called on to make such judgments consistently throughout a match. Your ability to do so is critical to the game and to your career as an official. Your competence in this area is directly tied to your overall competence as an official.

In theory, the ball-handling rule is a simple one: "Legal contact is a touch of the ball by a player's body above and including the waist which does not allow the ball to visibly come to rest or involve prolonged contact with a player's body." In reality, this rule results in some of the toughest calls you'll have to make as an official. Why? Because volleyball is a fast-paced game, and because every hit is a judgment call. Of course, many hits are easily seen as legal, and many are clearly illegal (we'll get into descriptions of legal and illegal hits in a moment). Those hits are easy to judge. But plenty of hits fall into a hazy borderline area, and these hits can pose nightmares for you if you aren't prepared to call them.

You need to know what constitutes a legal hit and what constitutes an illegal hit. You also need to know how to set a consistent standard in calling ball-handling violations, what to watch for and how to watch for it, in terms of player contacts, basic sets and keeping your focus in the proper place.

You'll learn about these things in this chapter, and your learning will be augmented by your experience on the court. As you gain experience, as you are able to maintain a consistent judgment standard and as you employ the techniques and tips presented here, you'll increase your competence in this most important area.

Legal and Illegal Hits

A legal hit occurs when a player contacts the ball with any part of his or her body above and including his or her waist, provided the ball doesn't visibly come to rest during the contact and it doesn't have prolonged contact with the player. This, of course, is the reverse of the description of an illegal hit, the rule for which was stated earlier.

A hit is legal if the ball contacts a legal part of the body that is in contact with a playable area of the floor, unless something about the contact makes it illegal, such as prolonged contact, multiple contact on the second or third hit, or the ball contacting the floor.

So what exactly is an illegal hit? Simply stated, a hit is illegal if

- the player has prolonged contact with the ball,
- the ball visibly comes to rest during the contact, or
- the ball contacts any body part below the waist.

When a player holds the ball, catches it, throws it or lifts or pushes it, this is considered illegal because the ball can be seen coming to rest. In addition, if a player contacts the ball twice in succession—either by hitting the ball twice in a row or by having the ball rebound from one part of the body to another on the same attempt—this is considered illegal. (In the latter example, however, note that a double hit is not illegal if it occurs on the first team hit or on a block.)

Although the definition of what is legal and what is illegal in ball handling can be put into words, the correct application of this rule is what makes for a successfully officiated match. Following are guidelines to use when determining legality:

- If the ball comes to a stop, such as when a player lifts the ball, this is considered a held ball.
- If the ball rolls up or down a player's arm or arms, this is considered illegal because the player has continued and steady contact with the ball. (However, if on the team's first contact the ball is not rolling but making a series of bounces, this is legal.)
- On a two-hand set, the hands must contact the ball simultaneously, except on the first team contact.
- The player's arm, forearm, hand or fist should not remain in contact with the ball when executing a spike; if it does, a throw is likely to result. Similarly, a block could become a throw or carry.
- When executing a tip or dump, the player's fingers cannot have prolonged contact with the ball. Watch for players who try to change

the direction of the ball by holding or guiding it during contact.

- A ball may be played off any body part above and including the waist. A ball hitting the chest is legal if it does not result in prolonged contact.
- Consider a pass a multiple contact if the contact is not simultaneous with the forearms, wrists or whatever body part is contacting the ball. The exception here is the team's first hit (by definition, it's still considered a multiple contact, but it is legal on any first contact).
- Using an underhand, palms-open technique does not necessarily result in an illegal hit.
- It is illegal for a player to carry the ball across the plane of her body, such as from right to left or from back to front.
- A ball that spins off the first pad of the fingers is probably legal; this is not considered "finger action."

A word of caution about hitting form: Sometimes a player looks awkward hitting the ball or uses poor technique or incorrect body position. Sometimes the ball spins in an unusual way or a play looks strange. None of this matters in making a judgment about whether the contact was legal. All that matters is the contact itself, based on the criteria you've just read.

Using Judgment

It's one thing to know the ball-handling rules; it's another to be a good judge of the action and to know when to call a violation. Your ability to exercise good judgment is based on your capacity for setting and maintaining a consistent standard, for using helpful techniques, for knowing where to focus and for understanding basic sets and player actions. In the rest of this chapter you'll learn about these aspects of judging contacts and knowing when to call ball-handling violations.

Setting a Consistent Standard

You might call a tight game, especially in terms of your ball-handling calls. Or you might be looser on your calls, allowing a margin for judgment error. Either approach will result in coaches and players complaining that your calls are too tight or too loose. Know that you're not going to please everyone with your calls—and of course, pleasing people shouldn't be your objective.

Your objective here should be to set a consistent standard for your calls, specifically your ball-handling calls. That standard must be based, of course, in the rules, but as mentioned, the rules for ball handling leave some leeway for interpretation. However you interpret the ball coming to rest or being held, and however you define prolonged contact, you must hold onto those interpretations and definitions, and you must call them the same way each time. The length of contact you allow should be the same for all ball-handling situations. When you operate in this manner, players know what to expect from you, what's allowed and what's not. The worst situation—and an unfair one to the players—is when you call it loose at the beginning of a match and then tighten up on your calls later on. When you change your standards, you open the door to justified criticism of your calling approach.

On the other hand, when you remain consistent with your calls, players will adjust. They'll quickly pick up that your calls are tight or loose or somewhere in between. The main point is that they'll know what to expect.

One last word about your judgment standard: If you're not certain a ball-handling violation occurred, don't call it. Give the players the benefit of the doubt. Call a violation only when you're sure of it. If, as a referee, you need help because you're screened from the action, get help from the umpire.

FIGURE 4.1   Officials' area of focus when watching for contact with the ball.

Judgment Techniques

Your ability to anticipate and focus is critical to your competence in making proper calls when ball-handling violations occur. *Don't follow the ball for its entire flight;* watch it just until it reaches the apex of its flight. At this point you'll know whether it is going to contact anything that would make it a dead ball. Once it's reached this point, shift your focus to where the ball is headed. The actions of the players in that area will tell you which player is going to receive it. Focus not just on that player, but on the player's body part that will play the ball (see figure 4.1). It's extremely important that you watch just the body part that is going to contact the ball; that's all that matters in terms of judging whether the contact is legal.

Remember that the better the players are, the faster the action is. You'll have little time to prepare between ball contacts. You'll need to be able to quickly shift your view from attacker to net to defense. Make sure you watch all of the attack; then shift to the net for a possible block and watch for contact there. If the ball goes beyond the blockers, shift to the area, as mentioned, where the ball is going. Home in on the player who is receiving it and the body part that it's being received with. Look ahead of the flight of the ball to the player, and have your eyes stationary and focused at the moment of contact.

Player Contacts and Basic Sets

Part of understanding the techniques and tactics executed by the players is in knowing the individual player actions used in contacting the ball and the basic sets a team uses. This knowledge helps you anticipate contacts and judge whether they're legal.

Player Contacts

Players can contact the ball in a number of ways. Each type of contact has its own inherent risks of becoming an illegal hit. Following are descriptions of the types of contacts and criteria for judging whether a ball-handling violation occurs during them.

Dump This skill is performed with the shoulders perpendicular to the net. Usually, the setter is trying to be deceptive by sending the ball across the net on the second hit instead of setting to the attacker for a third hit. It usually is kept very low so that after reacting to the surprise maneuver, the opponents will have little time to recover and make a strong offensive play.

Consider where the ball is initially contacted and where the ball goes. The setter cannot receive the ball on one side of the body and carry it across and release it on the other side of the body, as shown in figure 4.2. Doing so is considered a two-hand illegal dump. When the setter uses both hands, they must be in contact with the ball the same length of time. An example of a legal one-hand dump is shown in figure 4.3a; an example of a legal two-hand dump is shown in figure 4.3b.

Deep-Court Overhead Pass The deep-court overhead pass is performed by a skilled player from a poorly controlled pass. The player runs deep into the court and converts the ball to a front hitter or sends the ball over the net. Remember to judge the legality of the contact, not the technique.

Jump Set The setter performs the jump set in the air (see figure 4.4). It can be used for the purpose of deception, for a "quick" set or for maneuvering a bad pass into a useful set (usually one that is too close to the net), or it can be poor technique. Sometimes, instead of making the set at the

FIGURE 4.2   Two-hand illegal dump.

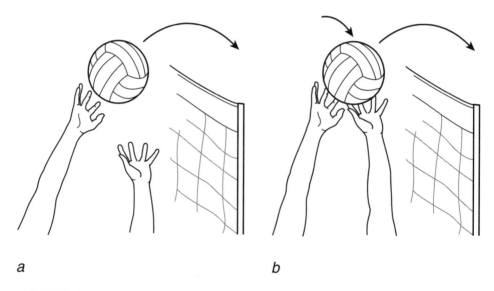

a   b

FIGURE 4.3   Legal dump: *(a)* one-hand; *(b)* two-hand.

height of the jump, the setter extends to set as her body is falling, often resulting in prolonged contact.

One-Hand Set   A setter may be forced to set the ball with one hand because the ball is being passed close to the net (see figure 4.5). Usually the setter is in the air and sets the middle for a quick attack. Remember to judge legality by length of contact, not technique.

FIGURE 4.4 Jump set.

FIGURE 4.5 One-hand set.

One-Hand Open Tip This skill is similar to the legal setting motion. The attacker executing the tip might disguise the action to look like a spike. At the height of the jump, the attacker will extend and reach with the attacking arm, extend or turn the wrist and direct the ball to an empty area on the court (see figure 4.6). The allowable length of time the hand can contact the ball is the same as in a legal set. Wrist action is essential in a proper set and therefore is permissible in the tipping action. However, the wrist action must be executed quickly enough to avoid prolonged contact with the ball; prolonged contact will result in a push, throw or carry.

FIGURE 4.6   One-hand open tip.

Most illegal tips occur when:

- the attacker does not execute the skill at the top of the jump,
- the player is out of position to play the ball,
- the ball is too low after the attacker jumps,
- the ball stays on the hand too long,
- direction is changed twice or
- the player carries the ball across the plane of the body.

Closed-Fist Tip   This is a rebounding skill in which a player bounces or punches the ball off her fisted hand (see figure 4.7). This is illegal only when the ball stays on the hand long enough to constitute a carry. The ball must be hit, not carried.

Spike   This can be performed open- or close-handed (see figure 4.8). The hand must contact the ball rapidly enough so the ball is hit, not thrown. A ball spiked with the top of the open hand (the fingers) might be a mis-hit rather than an illegal hit.

FIGURE 4.7   Closed-fist tip.

a

b

FIGURE 4.8   The spike: *(a)* open-hand; *(b)* closed-hand.

FIGURE 4.9　Backhand hit.

Backhand Hit　Usually this deceptive move is used by the spiker to change the obvious intended direction of the ball. The spiker jumps and hits the ball with the back of the hand (see figure 4.9). The ball must be hit, not pushed or thrown. The tendency is to push with the hand at the wrist like a wave. This hit also has the potential to create prolonged contact, but you will need to judge the contact, not the technique, to determine this.

Block　A block happens when a player(s) close to the net deflects the ball coming from the opponent by reaching higher than the top of the net; it can be done using either one or two hands (see figure 4.10). In either case, the blocker may not carry or have prolonged contact with the ball. Typically, a two-hand block has a natural

a

b

FIGURE 4.10　Blocks: *(a)* one-hand; *(b)* two-hand.

forward motion because blockers are taught to jump and penetrate the plane of the area above the net, whereas a one-hand block tends to have less motion of the arm. Also note that blocking techniques can involve wrist action.

Forearm Pass This passing skill is performed with the arms together and hands clasped or hands separated with simultaneous contact or with one hand or arm (see figure 4.11). The passer cannot have multiple contact with the ball except on one attempt to play the first team hit. Likewise, you should watch for prolonged contact with the ball.

Some illegal forearm passes occur when

- the ball contacts the area of the bent elbows and is held;
- the attempt is poorly timed, causing a lift;
- the ball rolls up or down the arms (prolonged contact); or
- the angle of execution results in a lift (e.g., the player is close to the net or has her back to the net).

a   b

FIGURE 4.11 Forearm pass: *(a)* two-arm, *(b)* one-arm.

Receiving With the Overhead Pass   Carefully observe a hard spiked or served ball received and converted by an overhead pass (see figure 4.12*a* and 4.12*b*). This pass is difficult and requires great strength on the part of the receiver to overcome the ball's forceful momentum and make a quick, snappy pass. The big risk here for the receiver is in holding the ball. This is especially true on hard-served balls. Also note that multiple contact on overhead finger action on first contact is allowed.

Also, watch for an overhead pass reception rolling back off one or both hands. Be sure you actually see prolonged contact on the serve reception before you call an illegal hit.

Soft Set   This set is characterized by a deep flex of the wrist, followed by extension and wrist snap (see figure 4.13*a* and 4.13*b*). Watch to determine whether the setter illegally lowers the ball excessively, such as to chest level, or receives the ball at a low chest level and snaps it away, which is legal. Any prolonged contact, of course, is illegal.

Remember, poor technique or mishandling the ball does not always result in illegal contact. Don't judge according to how unorthodox the play looks. Instead, watch the ball contact the hands.

Understanding Basic Sets

Generally, a team will use basic sets in a variety of ways. Understanding setting options helps you to prepare for the types of contacts setters will make and the types of contacts they are setting up for their teammates. Here are some basic sets to be aware of:

- *Quick set.* This set is about 1 foot above the net right next to the setter.
- *Low set.* This set goes 2 to 3 feet above the net, either in front of or behind the setter.
- *Normal outside set.* This set is directed toward the sideline, 4 to 8 feet above the net.
- *Shoot set.* This set travels quickly about 1 to 3 feet above the net. The hitter can contact the ball at various positions along the net inside the antennas.
- *Finger set.* This set is usually met and released with fingertip(s) above the setter's head and is the type of set that you will typically see from a setter. If this type of set comes from a libero who is on or in front of the attack line, an attack may not be completed if contact occurs while the ball is completely above the height of the net.

a

b

FIGURE 4.12   Receiving with an overhead pass.

a

b

FIGURE 4.13   Soft set.

Ball-handling judgment is at the core of good officiating. It takes time, patience, practice and experience. The keys are to know the rules, to stay up on techniques and tactics, to set a consistent judgment standard based on the rules and to know what to look for and when to look for it. When you know basic sets and the ins and outs of individual player contacts, and when you can stay a half step ahead of the action and focus on the body part of the player who is making the next contact, you're on your way to being a competent judge of ball handling.

CHAPTER 5

OFFENSIVE ALIGNMENTS AND OVERLAPPING AND SCREENING

As a volleyball official, you have a lot to look for in a fast-paced game in which players are always on the move. Just some of the situations you're watching for, in terms of their legality, are player alignments and overlapping, screening, serves, contacts, action near the center line and net and the movement of back-row players, including the libero player. You have to be keenly observant and know what to look for and where to look for it. As with ball-handling violations, you have to be a half step ahead of the action. If you aren't, you'll miss what just happened.

Two of those situations you need to be aware of—offensive alignments and overlapping, and screening—are the topics of this chapter. You'll explore various alignments and learn what to look for as far as potential violations are concerned. You'll learn about the potential for overlapping in various situations, and you'll examine how to determine when screening is occurring and when it is most likely to happen.

Offensive Alignments and Overlapping

Proper alignment occurs when all players, except the server positioned in the serving area, are in proper position within the team's playing area (the server is considered off the court and therefore is not part of the required alignment of players on the court). Players must be in correct serving order with no overlapping of adjacent players, either back to front or side to side, at the instant the server contacts the ball, as follows:

- *RB*: must be properly aligned with RF and CB.
- *RF*: must be properly aligned with CF and RB.

- *CF*: must be properly aligned with CB, LF and RF.
- *LF*: must be properly aligned with LB and CF.
- *LB*: must be properly aligned with LF and CB.
- *CB*: must be properly aligned with CF, LB and RB.

Recognizing Overlapping

How do you determine overlapping? As an official, your main area of focus when watching for overlapping should be on the position of the player's foot relative to the feet of the adjacent players, both side to side and back to front. You should consider only the foot or feet touching the floor when judging an overlap; that is, you should consider where a player's feet are in contact with the floor to determine their position in relation to adjacent players. Keep the following points in mind as you consider whether overlapping is occurring:

- Each right-side player must have at least part of one foot closer to the right sideline than both feet of the center player in the corresponding row (except the server and the center back of the serving team); see figure 5.1*a* for an example of a legal alignment and figure 5.1*b* for an example of an illegal alignment, which will result in a violation.

a   b

FIGURE 5.1   Right-side alignment: *(a)* legal alignment, in which right-side player is not overlapping with center player; *(b)* illegal alignment, in which right-side player is overlapping with center player.

- Each left-side player must have at least part of one foot closer to the left sideline than both feet of the center player in the corresponding row; see figure 5.2*a* for an example of a legal alignment and figure 5.2*b* for an example of an illegal alignment, which will result in a violation.
- Each front-row player must have at least part of one foot closer to the center line than both feet of the corresponding back-row player; see figure 5.3*a* for an example of a legal alignment and figure 5.3*b* for an example of an illegal alignment, which will result in a violation.

Also note that players can be moving prior to the serve, and they may have any part of the body on the boundary lines at the time of the serve. However, no part of the body can be touching the floor outside those lines at the moment the server contacts the ball. After the server contacts the ball, players can move from their respective positions.

a   *b*

FIGURE 5.2   Left-side alignment: *(a)* legal alignment, in which left-side player is not overlapping with center player; *(b)* illegal alignment, in which left-side player is overlapping with center player.

a   b

FIGURE 5.3   Front-row alignment: *(a)* legal alignment, in which front-row player is not overlapping with back-row player; *(b)* illegal alignment, in which front-row player is overlapping with back-row player.

Potential for Overlapping

The potential for player overlapping occurs as teams adjust player positions to enhance team passing, facilitate smoother setter-to-hitter transitions, or try to disguise their attack. The diagrams throughout the rest of this section show various team serve–receive systems and possible overlapping situations created by each system.

4-2 Offense   In the 4-2 offensive pattern, the setter always comes from the front row. Watch for possible overlap of these players:

- The setter (LF) and the center-front (CF), as shown in figure 5.4*a*
- The setter (CF) and the right-front (RF), as shown in figure 5.4*b*
- The left-back (LB) and the CB, as shown in figure 5.4*c*
- The setter (RF) and the CF and the CF and the CB, as shown in figure 5.4*d*

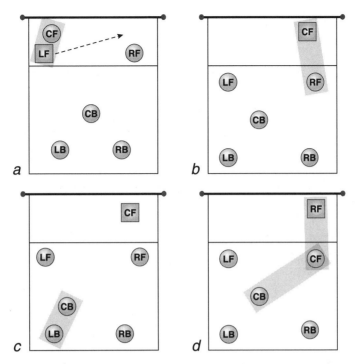

FIGURE 5.4   Possible areas for overlap in 4-2 offense.

6-2 Offense   In the 6-2 offensive pattern, the setters always come from the back row. Watch for overlap of the following players in a 6-2 offense with three serve receivers:

- The RF and the setter (RB) and the LF and the CF, as shown in figure 5.5a
- The setter (CB) and the CF and the CB and RB, as shown in figure 5.5b
- The setter (LB) and the LF and the LB and the CB, as shown in figure 5.5c

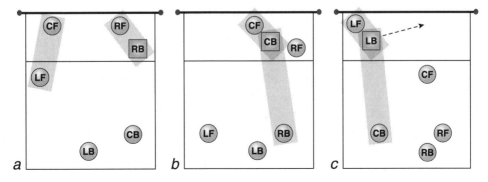

FIGURE 5.5   Possible areas for overlap in 6-2 offense with three serve receivers.

Watch for overlap of these players in a 6-2 offense with four serve receivers:

- The CF and RF and the setter (RB) and the CB, as shown in figure 5.6*a*
- The setter (CB) and RB, as shown in figure 5.6*b*
- The setter (LB) and CB and the LF and the CF, as shown in figure 5.6*c*

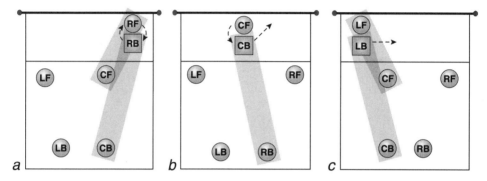

FIGURE 5.6   Possible areas for overlap in 6-2 offense with four serve receivers.

Decoys

Teams may use decoys to hide the setter, thus disguising their attack and hoping to catch the opponents off guard. Decoys present situations of possible overlap because the players involved in the decoy might move too early to get to their positions, or they might align themselves incorrectly to begin with. Watch for overlap of these players when decoys are used:

- The LF and CF and the setter (RF) and the RB, as shown in figure 5.7*a*
- The setter (CF) and RF, as shown in figure 5.7*b*

In figure 5.7*a*, the setter is acting as a decoy before the opponent serves the ball. The setter wants to make the opposing team think there are three spikers on the front row—in other words, that she is a hitter, not a setter. The CB will often fake a spike from this formation, which allows the setter the option of spiking, dumping or setting.

Teams will occasionally use a hidden setter as a decoy from any front-row position. If a team uses a hidden setter from the CF position, as shown in figure 5.7*b*, the CB usually fakes a spike, but cannot legally spike the ball.

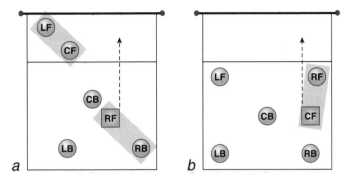

FIGURE 5.7 Possible areas for overlap when decoys are used.

5-1 Offense

In the 5-1 offense, the setter is always the same player. Watch for overlap of the following players in a 5-1 offense (note that these diagrams show a 5-1 offense in which the setter is in the back row. For examples of a 5-1 offense in which the setter is in the front row, see figure 5.7 in the preceding section):

- The setter (CB) and CF and CB and RB, as shown in figure 5.8*a*
- The LF and the setter (LB) and the CB and LB, as shown in figure 5.8*b*

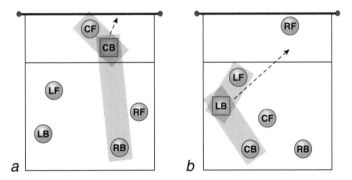

FIGURE 5.8 Possible areas for overlap in a 5-1 offense.

Two-Player Receive/5-1 Offense

In this offense, the same two players are designed to receive the serve every time. The back-row players not passing (except the setter) stand close to the end line to assist passers in determining in and out balls. The front-row players stand close to the net to give passers the full use of the court.

The two players designated as the passers are directly opposite each other, so one is always a front-row player and the other is always a back-row player. Possible overlaps in this offense are shown in figures 5.9*a* through 5.9*f*:

- The LF and LB and the CB and RB, as shown in figure 5.9*a*
- The CF and CB and the CB and the setter (RB), as shown in figure 5.9*b*
- The CF and the setter (CB) and the CF and RF, as shown in figure 5.9*c*
- The setter (LB) and LF and LF and CF, as shown in figure 5.9*d*
- The CF and CB and the RF and CF, as shown in figure 5.9*e*
- The setter (CF) and RF, as shown in figure 5.9*f*

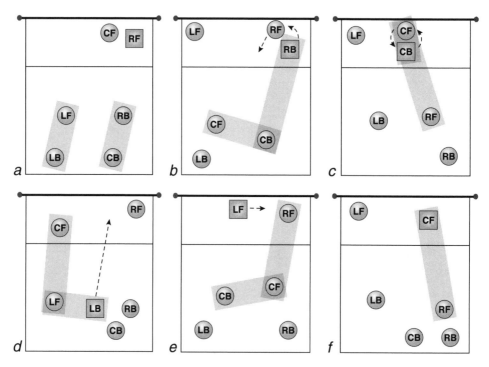

FIGURE 5.9   Possible areas for overlap in a two-player receive/5-1 offense.

Four-Player Receive/Front-Row Setter

In a four-player receive with a front-row setter, four players are set up to receive the serve. Possible overlaps in this offense are shown in figures 5.10*a* through 5.10*c*.

- The setter (LF) moves to the right side of the court near the net, and the CF moves to the middle to hit and block there. The RF moves left and hits and blocks left. The setter will block right. In this system, there's a possible overlap between the LF and CF, as shown in figure 5.10*a*.

- On the serve, the front-row setter (CF) moves to her area, while the RF stays to block middle and the LF hits and blocks left. The setter still blocks right. In this setup, there is possible overlap between the CF and RF as shown in figure 5.10*b*.

- The setter (RF) moves to the target area, the LF moves in to hit middle and the CF moves to the left to hit and block. In this formation, a possible overlap exists between the RF and CF, as shown in figure 5.10*c*.

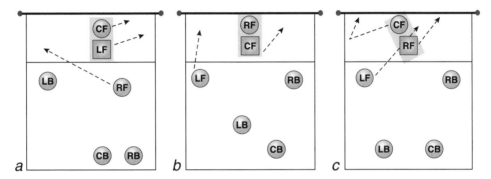

FIGURE 5.10   Possible areas for overlap in a four-player receive/front-row setter offense.

Four-Player Receive/Back-Row Setter

The possibility for overlap exists in a four-player receive with a back-row setter, too. Possible overlaps in this offense are shown in figures 5.11*a* through 5.11*c*.

- The setter (LB) moves two-thirds of the way across the court to the right, near the net, while the LF moves to hit and block middle and the CF, in serve–receive position, moves to hit left. The RF moves to hit right. The setter usually plays defense in the RB position. Possible overlaps here include between the setter and the CB, as shown in figure 5.11*a*, and between the LF and CF, as shown in figure 5.11*b*.

- At the moment of the serve, the setter (RB) moves to the two-thirds position, the CF hits middle, the LF hits left and the RF hits right. The setter plays defense in the RB position. The potential for overlap exists between the setter and RF, as shown in figure 5.11*c*.

- At the moment of the serve, the setter (CB) moves to position, the RF moves quickly to hit middle, the CF slides along the net and out to hit right and the LF hits left. When there is a lot of movement, such as in this situation, there is a great potential for overlap. Overlap in this situation can occur between the setter and the CF, as shown in figure 5.11*d*, the setter and the RF, as shown in figure 5.11*e*, and the setter and the RB, as shown in figure 5.11*f*.

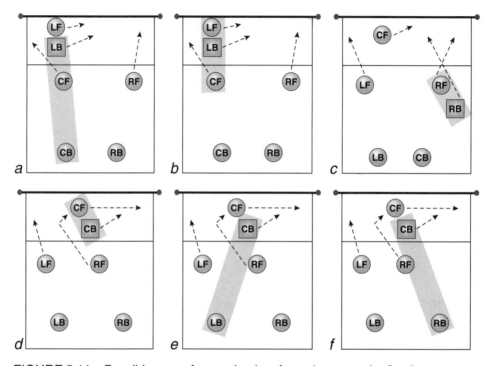

FIGURE 5.11   Possible areas for overlap in a four-player receive/back-row setter offense.

Stack-Left Offense

This formation is often used to position the setter closer to the target area for passing. When the LB is the setter, the RB will at times run a fake attack. The front row can run a variety of hitting patterns and sets in this offense. Possible overlaps in this offense are shown in figures 5.12*a* and 5.12*b*:

- The setter (LB) and CB and LB and LF, as shown in figure 5.12*a*
- The CB and CF and the CB and RB, as shown in figure 5.12*b*

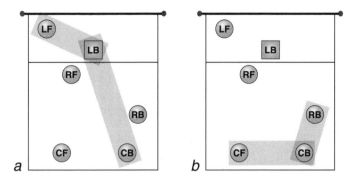

FIGURE 5.12   Possible areas for overlap in a stack-left offense.

Stack-Right Offense

This formation is often used to improve passing from the serve–receive positions. Possible overlaps in this offense are shown in figures 5.13*a* and 5.13*b*.

- The LB and LF and the LF and CF, as shown in figure 5.13*a*
- The CF and CB and the CF and the setter (RF), as shown in figure 5.13*b*

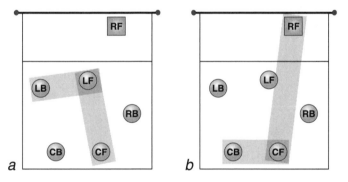

FIGURE 5.13   Possible areas for overlap in a stack-right offense.

3-5 Switch/CF-LB Switch

To improve back-row passing, the CF and LB (the #3 and #5 players) might switch positions. A team typically uses this switch when the setter is in the RB position. Possible overlaps in this situation are shown in figures 5.14*a* and 5.14*b*.

- The LF and LB and the LF and CF, as shown in figure 5.14*a*
- The CB and CF and the CB and the setter (RB), as shown in figure 5.14*b*

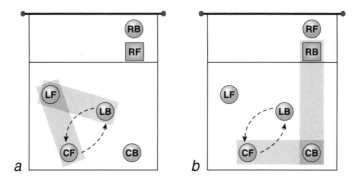

FIGURE 5.14   Possible areas for overlap in a 3-5 switch/CF-LB switch.

1-3 Switch/RB-CF Switch

Another formation used to improve passing is the 1-3 switch, in which the RB and CF (the #1 and #3 players) exchange positions on the court. Teams typically use this switch when the setter is coming from the LB position. Possible overlaps in this situation are shown in figures 5.15a through 5.15c.

- The CB and the setter (LB), as shown in figure 5.15a
- The CB and CF, as shown in figure 5.15b
- The CF and RF, as shown in figure 5.15c

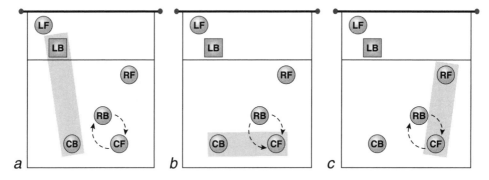

FIGURE 5.15   Possible areas for overlap in a 1-3 switch/RB-CF switch.

Screening

Players on the serving team shall not take action to prevent receivers from seeing the contact of the serve or the path of the served ball. Teams use screening techniques as an offensive strategy to keep the receiving team from a clear view of the serve. Perhaps the strategy is in response to an increased proficiency in serve receiving in general. Whatever the reason, screening is illegal, and you need to have a clear understanding of the screening rule to ensure fair play. Essentially, the rule states that screening is an action that prevents receivers from seeing the contact of the serve and the flight of the served ball.

Because players on the receiving team are only assured the right to see the contact of the served ball and the path of the served ball, there are few instances in which you can automatically call a screen. You should be aware, however, of several situations in which potential screens exist. Part of your obligation here is to make sure that the limited rights of the receiving team are not further restricted by the serving team. Potential screens exist when

- a player on the serving team raises or waves her arms;
- a player on the serving team jumps or moves sideways just before the service is executed, and the ball is served directly over that player;
- two or more teammates stand in close proximity, and the ball is served directly over them or
- two or more players are not standing close together, but they are stacked between the server and the receivers.

As an official, you will need to weigh the following factors when you're judging whether a screen has been committed:

- Relative positions on the serving team
- Path of the serve
- Speed of the serve
- Trajectory of the serve

If the players of the serving team are positioned close to each other and a fast serve with a low trajectory passes over these players, the probability is greater that a screen has been committed than if the serve is slow and high. Conversely, the probability that a screen has been committed is lower if the players are not positioned close to each other or are attempting to prevent a screen (e.g., bending over); if the path of the serve is not over the players; if the speed of the serve is slow or if the trajectory of the serve is high.

Another factor that makes screens difficult to call is the fact that no player on the receiving team is entitled to a specific position on the floor. If a player on the receiving team cannot see the server, that player should move. If, after that player moves, the serving team's player moves to take another position that blocks that player's view of the serve, you should call screening.

The screening rule is in place to give the defense a fair chance to receive the serve. But players on both sides of the net have an obligation to keep the situation legal—and you have an obligation to call screening if, after you've considered all the salient factors, the situation is not legal.

This wraps up the section on mechanics. You've learned about your prematch, match, and postmatch responsibilities; ball-handling violations and, in this chapter, offensive alignments and overlapping and screening. Continue to study your rules book and to learn from firsthand experience and secondhand observation; your knowledge of, and ability to execute, the mechanics of officiating are the keys to your success as a volleyball official.

PART III

APPLYING THE RULES

CHAPTER 6

THE GAME, COURT, EQUIPMENT AND UNIFORMS

As you know from your rules book, there are 12 main areas of rules:

- Rule 1: The Game
- Rule 2: The Court
- Rule 3: Game Equipment
- Rule 4: Player Equipment and Uniform
- Rule 5: Officials: Responsibilities and Positions
- Rule 6: The Team: Composition and Positions
- Rule 7: Roster and Lineup
- Rule 8: The Serve
- Rule 9: During Play
- Rule 10: Substitution and Libero Replacement
- Rule 11: Time-Outs and Intermission
- Rule 12: Conduct

In the next three chapters we'll consider various cases involving those 12 rules. For each rule we'll present several cases; at the chapter's end we'll provide the appropriate rulings. The references to the rules, of course, are meant to supplement your close study of the rules book and help bring to life some of the situations you will face. By no means are these discussions meant to substitute for a thorough study of the rules book. Make sure you are well versed in all the rules as spelled out in the rules book, and then use chapters 6 through 8 to test and augment your understanding of them.

In this chapter we'll consider cases in the first four rules:

- Rule 1: The Game
- Rule 2: The Court
- Rule 3: Game Equipment
- Rule 4: Player Equipment and Uniform

Rule 1: The Game

Rule 1 covers three aspects of the game: the coin toss, suspended play and forfeited play and the length of the game. Here we'll present three cases and answers based on their rulings. Consider how you'd respond in each case, and then check your rulings against those in the "Appropriate Rulings" section at the end of the chapter.

CASE 1: Interrupted Rally

A long rally in the fourth game of a match between Jamestown and Pittsfield is interrupted when the gym lights go out. How do you rule?

Would your ruling be any different if one light fixture shattered, but the other lights remained on? How would you rule if the net cable were to break?

CASE 2: Delayed Game

Brownsburg, hosting York in a dual match, has only five players at game time. The Brownsburg coach calls a time-out to give her players more time to reach the court. How do you rule?

CASE 3: Best Two of Three?

Centralia is playing a varsity match at Westwood. Prior to the match, both head coaches approach you, saying they have agreed to play a two-of-three match, rather than the customary three-of-five match. Do you allow this?

Rule 2: The Court

This rule guides you in making judgments regarding court markings, overhead obstructions, out-of-bounds situations and restricted play cases. Read the following cases, decide how you'd respond and check your rulings against those at the end of the chapter.

CASE 4: Center-Line Dilemma

Richmond is preparing to play a match at Independence. As you inspect the court before the match begins, you note that the center line is not continuous; the Independence mascot is painted on the floor in the center of the court, obliterating a portion of the center line. What do you do?

1. Leave the court as it is and do nothing about the missing center line.
2. Correct the court only if the Richmond coach protests, by having the Independence management tape the line over the mascot.
3. Correct the court regardless of any protest, by having the Independence management tape the line over the mascot.
4. Forfeit the match to Richmond.

CASE 5: Overhead Obstruction

Brownsburg is playing at Jamestown when Brownsburg's CB, in receiving a serve, volleys the ball so that it hits an overhead obstruction on Brownsburg's side of the net. The obstruction is over an area that is 10 feet outside the playing area of the court. Brownsburg's RF makes the team's second hit, successfully volleying the ball over the net.

What's your ruling? Is this legal? Would your ruling be any different if the obstruction were only 5 feet outside the playing area of the court?

CASE 6: Out of Bounds?

Pittsfield is playing at York. A Pittsfield player hits a softly looping ball that strikes a basketball backboard that is hanging in a vertical position in the playable area behind Pittsfield's court. The ball drops to the floor, out of bounds, on Pittsfield's side. What should happen?

Would your response be any different if the backboard were hanging over Pittsfield's court, instead of behind it? What if the backboard were hanging in a nonplayable area above the bleachers?

CASE 7: Player Stepping on Bleachers

A Richmond player, in a game against Westwood, makes a spectacular save of an errant pass by a teammate. At contact of the ball, she has one foot on the first row of the bleachers and one foot on the floor. She passes back to a teammate for a third hit, which goes successfully over the net. The bleachers are 5 feet from the sideline. Is this legal, and do you allow play to continue?

Would your response be different if the bleachers were 6 or more feet from the sideline?

Rule 3: Game Equipment

Rule 3 details the specifications of various pieces of equipment, including the covering and padding of net cables, the legality of the net system, the referee platform, the official scoresheet, the officials' table and the team benches. Place yourself in the role of the referee and decide how you'd respond in the following cases. Then check your rulings against those at the end of the chapter.

CASE 8: Faulty Net System
Before a match pitting Independence against Centralia, you notice that the net system does not include cables or ropes through the bottom of the net. It does have a cable through the top of the net. Can the match be played, or does the bottom of the net need to have a rope or cable through it first?

CASE 9: Inadequate Referee Platform
You arrive at the York gym for a match between Jamestown and York. As you are inspecting the court and the game equipment, you note that the referee platform is not high enough; your head will not be 2 to 3 feet above the top of the net when you are on the platform. What do you do? Can the match be forfeited to Jamestown if York doesn't fix the problem?

What if the platform were high enough, but you deemed it unstable and unsafe? What if there were no platform at all, but just a folding ladder or a chair?

CASE 10: Officials' Table Too Close to Court
Upon inspecting the court prior to a match between Pittsfield and Browns-burg, you note that, as a result of the structure of the facility, the officials' table is 4 feet from the sideline, rather than the minimum 6 feet. The Pittsfield coach notices this as well and says that Brownsburg should be required to forfeit the match because the table puts her players (as well as the Brownsburg players) in jeopardy. How do you rule?

Rule 4: Player Equipment and Uniform

This rule clarifies legality issues concerning the equipment and uniforms of players. Because numerous situations can and do arise regarding equipment and uniforms, make sure you're well versed in this rule, and make your judgments accordingly. Consider how you'd judge in the following cases, and then check your rulings against those in the next section.

CASE 11: Hand Cast
Centralia is playing a dual match at Richmond. Midway through the first game, a Centralia substitute is about to enter the game. You notice that she has a padded cast on her hand. Do you allow her to enter?

Would your decision be any different if the player were wearing a flexible plastic support on her forearm? What if she were wearing a thick layer of sweatbands on her forearm?

CASE 12: Player Wearing Jewelry

As you conduct the prematch conference before a match between West-wood and Independence, you discover that the Independence captain is wearing tongue jewelry. What is your ruling in this situation? What if you noticed another player with jewelry on during warm-ups?

CASE 13: Tie-Dyed Shirts

Richmond shows up at Jamestown for a match with tie-dyed uniform tops. The numbers are clearly visible and have a quarter-inch shadow on one side. Is this legal?

Would your ruling be any different if the numbers blended in with the colors of the uniform tops? How about if the numbers were made up of three digits on each uniform?

CASE 14: Mismatched Undershirts

As you watch Independence and Pittsfield warm up prior to their match, you notice that Pittsfield players are wearing shirts under their sleeve-less red uniform tops. Some of the players are wearing short-sleeved undershirts, and some are wearing long-sleeved undershirts. All of the undershirts are red. Is this legal?

Would your ruling be any different if some of the players had red undershirts and some had white undershirts?

CASE 15: Libero Uniform

Pittsfield's libero enters the warm-up wearing her libero uniform, which is light yellow. The regular players for Pittsfield are wearing an off-white uniform. All numbers are legal. What is your ruling concerning the legal-ity of the color of the libero's uniform?

Answers

Here we've provided the appropriate ruling to each case in this chapter. Check your responses to see how you did.

Case 1: Interrupted Rally

If the lights in the gym go out, you should suspend the game and resume it with a replay as soon as the situation is corrected. If it can't be corrected in a timely manner to resume the game during the scheduled time, then the rest of the match should be rescheduled. However, check with your state association because they may have rules that address this differ-ently than the NFHS.

The same response is appropriate in the cases of a light fixture shat-tering or a net cable breaking. In unusual situations such as these, you need to use common sense so both teams remain relaxed and neither suffers a disadvantage.

Case 2: Delayed Game

In order for the game to begin each team must have six eligible players on the court. The rules allow a time-out to be called prior to the start of the game, so the time-out would be granted. If the six players were still not on the court after the time-out was taken, forfeiture of the match would be declared. (However, it is important that every effort within the rules be made to have the contest before calling forfeiture, especially when teams have traveled to play.)

Case 3: Best Two of Three?

A standard match uses the three-of-five format. The only way the three-of-five format can be altered to a two-of-three format is if the state association has adopted the option to use the two-of-three format for match competition at the varsity level. This is not a decision to be made on site by mutual agreement. Respective state-association adoptions should be followed and coaches and officials should be clear on these adoptions to avoid on-site confusion.

Case 4: Center-Line Dilemma

Answer 3 is correct: You should have the Independence management tape the line over the mascot. You should not let the situation go; the center line needs to be solid and continuous, or a shadow-bordered 2-inch-wide line, and it must extend the width of the court. It doesn't matter whether a coach protests; you need to ensure that the line is in place before the match begins.

Case 5: Overhead Obstruction

The play is legal. The play would also be legal if the overhead obstruction were only 5 feet (and not 10 feet) outside the playing area of the court. The only salient points about where the ball strikes the overhead obstruction are which side of the court the obstruction is on and whether it is above a playable area. Because Brownsburg hit the ball, and the ball hit an overhead obstruction above a playable area on their side, they can continue to play the ball. If the ball struck an obstruction on the Jamestown side, a Brownsburg player could not be the next player to contact the ball.

Case 6: Out of Bounds?

The ball should be replayed if it hits a backboard that is in a playable area behind Pittsfield's court—and if you determine that the ball would have remained in play had it not hit the backboard. Obviously, this is a judgment call that you have to make.

The ball should also be replayed if it hits a backboard hanging over Pittsfield's court, and again you determine that the ball would have remained in play had the backboard not been there.

If, however, the ball hits a backboard in a nonplayable area above the bleachers, you should award a point to York.

Case 7: Player Stepping on Bleachers

You allow play to continue. However, because the bleachers are only 5 feet from the sidelines, if the player did not successfully play the ball, you should call a replay.

Players may play a ball over a nonplayable area if they have one part of their body in contact with the playable area. They may also continue into the nonplayable area after making contact. In this situation, if the bleachers, which are 5 feet from the court, cause the player to be unsuccessful in playing the ball back and you judge that the player could have made a play had the bleachers not been there, you can call for a replay.

Case 8: Faulty Net System

The match can be played without a cable or rope through the bottom of the net—provided the net meets all other rule specifications, including the entire net remaining taut at the specified height. This situation should be reported to the state association.

Case 9: Inadequate Referee Platform

You should immediately notify the home management (York) of the problem, and they should do all they can to provide you with a safe, stable platform that elevates you to a height where your head will be 2 to 3 feet above the top of the net.

However, if the situation can't be rectified by match time, or if you deem the platform to be unsafe, you can officiate from the floor if necessary. In this case, you should notify the state association after the match, but the match should be played.

Case 10: Officials' Table Too Close to Court

Although the rules state that the officials' table should be at least 6 feet from the sideline, and preferably at least 10 feet away, you should not penalize Brownsburg in this situation because the short distance between the table and the sideline is the result of the structure of the facility. Instead, you should make appropriate calls when a player's effort to legally play the ball or a player's safety is affected. In this type of situation, the front edge of the officials' table should be padded.

Case 11: Hand Cast

It's not legal for a player to wear a padded cast on her hand in competition. This is considered illegal equipment, and you should assess Centralia an unnecessary delay and not allow the player to enter.

You should make the same ruling if the player attempts to enter with a flexible plastic support on her forearm. However, you should not assess a team delay if she has a thick layer of sweatbands on her arm. She can enter the game.

Case 12: Player Wearing Jewelry

Tongue jewelry is considered illegal equipment, so players may not wear it during the warm-up or game. Since you discovered the tongue jewelry during the prematch conference (before warm-ups), there is no penalty and you should ask that it be removed. If the jewelry is discovered during warm-ups, you should direct the player to remove it. There is no penalty unless the player does not comply with your request, in which case it would be considered unsporting conduct.

If the jewelry had been discovered during the game, you would assess an unnecessary delay against Independence. Once the player removes the tongue jewelry, she is allowed to play. If a player sitting on the bench is wearing jewelry during a game, there would be no penalty assessed unless she attempts to enter the game while wearing it. As soon as you notice jewelry being worn by a player on the bench, it is good preventive officiating to notify the coach and request the player remove it. An even better preventive practice is to remind players and coaches to remove any illegal equipment before warm-ups begin.

Case 13: Tie-Dyed Shirts

There is no penalty if the tie-dyed shirts have clearly visible numbers with a shadow. If, however, the numbers are made up of triple digits, or blend in with the uniform tops, that would be illegal. In the case of illegal team uniforms, the match would begin with Jamestown being awarded a point. You should notify the state association after the match.

Case 14: Mismatched Undershirts

It is legal for some players to wear short-sleeved undershirts while some of their teammates wear long-sleeved undershirts, as long as the undershirts are the same color and that color is similar to the dominant color of their uniforms.

However, teammates can't wear different-colored undershirts. So in the second example, the players with the white undershirts would need to replace them with red ones of the same color as their teammates before entering the game. Another option is that the entire team can play without undershirts.

Case 15: Libero Uniform

The libero uniform must be immediately recognized as being distinct from the other players' uniforms. Light yellow and off-white are not clearly distinguishable from each other and should be considered illegal.

CHAPTER 7

OFFICIALS AND TEAMS

In chapter 6 you considered cases concerning the first four rule categories, including the game, the court, equipment and uniforms. In this chapter we'll move on to the following rules:

- Rule 5: Officials: Responsibilities and Positions
- Rule 6: The Team: Composition and Positions
- Rule 7: Roster and Lineup

As in chapter 6, read each case, decide how you would rule, and then check your rulings against those in the "Appropriate Rulings" section at the end of the chapter.

Rule 5: Officials: Responsibilities and Positions

Rule 5 focuses on the responsibilities of all the officials: the referee, the umpire, the scorer, the assistant scorer, the timer and the line judges. Chapters 2 and 3 were devoted to detailing all the officials' duties; here you can test your recall ability as you consider some cases related to those responsibilities.

CASE 1: Illegal Replacement
Upon rotation to serve, team Ruthville's libero is replaced by a player other than the player for whom the libero entered the game. Ruthville then serves for three points before the assistant scorer realizes there has been an illegal replacement. How would you correct this error? What if Ruthville's next serve goes into the net and there is a loss of rally to the opponent before this is discovered and reported to you?

CASE 2: Missed Call?
After a long and well-played rally between Brownsburg and Centralia, which Brownsburg wins, the Centralia coach brings to your attention

the fact that a back-row player from Brownsburg completed a block. What do you do?

CASE 3: Wrong Serving Order

York serves a ball into the net in a game against Westwood and then calls a time-out. When both teams return to the floor, the Westwood coach asks for a lineup check for their team. The umpire places Westwood in an improper serving order. Westwood goes on to win four straight points before York regains the serve. At this point the scorer notifies the umpire that Westwood has been in improper serving order during the four points that they just scored. What should you, as referee, do?

CASE 4: Premature Celebrating?

In the final game of its match against Pittsfield, Jamestown apparently scores game point, thus winning the game and the match. The Jamestown players and coaches run onto the court in celebration. However, as the umpire checks the score, he realizes that Jamestown has only 14 points, not 15. How do you, as referee, handle this situation?

CASE 5: Scorer Error?

The York coach requests a 19th team substitution in a match against Brownsburg. When penalized for the illegal substitution, the York coach complains that she wasn't told of her team's 15th through 18th substitutions and wasn't aware that it was the 19th. Is this a valid complaint? Should York not be penalized for illegal substitution?

Rule 6: The Team: Composition and Positions

This rule clarifies issues surrounding team players, captains, alignments and screening. Try your hand at the cases presented, and then check your rulings against those in the "Answers" section later in the chapter.

CASE 6: No Captain on the Court

In a game against Westwood, the Centralia playing captain departs for a substitution. The Centralia coach forgets to designate a new playing captain on the court. What are the ramifications of this? Should Centralia be penalized in any way?

CASE 7: Incorrect Server

Although no one catches it at the time, an incorrect server scores two points for Richmond in a game against Independence. When Independence regains the serve, its server is about to serve and is granted a re-serve after making a bad toss. Before the Independence server makes contact with the ball to put it in play, the scorer discovers that Richmond scored its last two points with an incorrect server. The scorer brings this to your attention. What should happen here?

CASE 8: Playing With Five Players

Brownsburg, playing at Jamestown, has only six players. One player is injured and cannot play the rest of the match. Does Brownsburg have to forfeit the match?

CASE 9: Screen?

Pittsfield is about to serve to York. As the Pittsfield server prepares to serve, the three front-row players for Pittsfield are grouped together. The ball is served over the CB and CF, who are bent at the waist. Is this screening?

Would your judgment be different if the ball were served in a high looping trajectory? What if it were served fast and hard, but you believed the receivers could see the contact of the serve and the flight of the ball?

Rule 7: Roster and Lineup

Rule 7 delves into roster and lineup issues, including the number of players, eligible and ineligible players, adding players to the roster and incorrect lineups. Respond to the following cases and see how you did by checking your rulings against those at the end of the chapter.

CASE 10: Lineup Submission

The Brownsburg coach submits a lineup, but fails to indicate the intention to use the libero for that game. What would you do if you discovered this with only five minutes remaining in the prematch warm-up? What would you do if you did not discover this until you were checking the lineup on the court to start the game?

CASE 11: Wrong Uniform Number

Five minutes before the end of the prematch warm-up prior to a match between Westwood and Richmond, the scorer discovers that Richmond has the wrong uniform number listed for one of its players. What should happen here? Would your response be any different if the scorer had discovered that Richmond had an unlisted team member?

CASE 12: Adding Names to the Roster

Three minutes before the end of the prematch warm-up, Independence, which is due to serve first in its match against Centralia, presents its roster and lineup to the scorer. Then, 30 seconds before the end of the prematch warm-up, Independence presents two additional names for its roster. How do you respond?

CASE 13: Changing Uniform Numbers

A teammate's errant elbow at the net results in a bloody nose for a Jamestown player in a match against York. Excessive blood drips onto the player's uniform top, but the bleeding is stopped fairly quickly. The Jamestown coach substitutes for the player and instructs him to go to the locker room and take off his bloody uniform top—#2—and put on his teammate's uniform top, which has #15 on it. The original #15 player will wear a T-shirt and won't play in the match.

Is this legal? Can the Jamestown player switch his uniform top (and number) and reenter the game?

CASE 14: Number Mix-Up

Just as a match between Pittsfield and Brownsburg is about to start, you discover that there is a player #22 listed on Pittsfield's lineup sheet, but player #12 is on the court and player #22 is on the bench. What should happen? Should Pittsfield be penalized?

CASE 15: Libero Position

Upon loss of rally, Ruthville's libero erroneously rotates to the LF position. Immediately after her teammate serves an ace, the libero tracker notifies the umpire that the libero should have been replaced rather than rotated to the front row. What is the call? What should the umpire do?

CASE 16: Libero Setting the Ball

The Westwood libero, at the net, overhead finger-sets the ball to her hitter, who contacts the ball while completely above the height of the net. The attacked ball is legally blocked by a York player. Does play continue? If not, what is the call?

CASE 17: Libero Serving

Following Bismarck's #5 serves, their libero (#1) replaces #5 to play the back row. After three rotations, Bismarck gets the side-out and rotates to serve. The libero, who was playing in the left-back position in place of #5, rotates directly to the serving position to replace Bismarck's #10 who is coming from the right-front position to the right-back (serving) position. Bismarck's #5 returns to the game at the left-front position and #10 leaves the court. Should the rule requiring a play between replacements be enforced in this situation?

Answers

In this section you'll find the correct rulings for the cases in this chapter. Check these against your rulings to see how you did.

Case 1: Illegal Replacement

Because Ruthville scored three points while an illegal player was on the court, those points would be deleted from the scoresheet and a loss of rally would be administered. If the wrong replacement is not noticed and brought to your attention until after Ruthville loses serve, the points may be deleted from the scoresheet up until the opponent's contact for serve.

Case 2: Missed Call?

You should briefly confer with the umpire. If neither you nor the umpire saw a back-row violation, the point stands. If the umpire confirms that he saw a violation, then you should negate the point given to Brownsburg and award it, and the serve, to Centralia instead. This is admittedly not a desirable situation for an official, but the ultimate responsibility is to get it right.

Case 3: Wrong Serving Order

You should cancel the four points that Westwood scored when they were in the wrong serving order. You can't allow points to be scored with an improper server. In conferring with the umpire, you should correct the serving order, take away the four points and give the ball to Westwood, this time with the proper server serving.

It's appropriate to correct errors made by members of the officiating crew, as long as the correction happens before the opposing team contacts the ball for serve.

Case 4: Premature Celebrating?

First, you should give the end-of-game signal and direct the teams to report to their respective end lines. Then, after you confirm that the game is not over, the same six players that were on the court for Jamestown should reenter the court in the same serving order, and Jamestown should serve again. (Jamestown can make a substitution before the serve, as long as it is done within the rules.)

If a team continues to forget the end-of-game procedures, it could be considered unsporting behavior and penalized as such. Preventive officiating calls for the umpire to be aware of when game point arises, and to signal game point at the appropriate time.

Case 5: Scorer Error?

The York coach does not have a valid complaint; her team is guilty of an illegal substitution. It is ultimately the coach's responsibility to know how many substitutions her team has made.

Case 6: No Captain on the Court

Centralia is not penalized for not having a playing captain on the court, but no Centralia player can request a time-out or a check of the serving order, or otherwise communicate with officials. Only a playing captain (among the players) can do this. When the umpire realizes there is no captain on the court, he or she should request that the Centralia coach designate a playing captain. The scorer should work closely with the umpire to prevent this situation from occurring.

Case 7: Incorrect Server

You should cancel the points scored by Richmond's improper server because the Independence server hadn't served yet. Although the Independence server had made a bad toss in attempting to serve, he hadn't yet contacted the ball to put it into play. Had he contacted the ball to put it into play, the points scored by Richmond's improper server couldn't be canceled.

Case 8: Playing With Five Players

No, Brownsburg doesn't have to forfeit the match. They can play with five players. Each time the injured player's position—the now-vacant position—rotates to the RB position, Brownsburg has a loss of rally, and Jamestown is awarded the ball and gets to serve.

Case 9: Screen?

None of the examples are screens. If the server had served fast and hard, and you believed the receivers couldn't see the contact or the flight of the ball, that would have been screening.

If a ball is served high and is easy to react to, don't call a screen, regardless of the position of the players on the serving team. Likewise, if the serving team players attempt to give the receivers a view of the service contact (by bending at the waist), don't call a screen. In general, if you believe the receivers had a view of the contact of the serve, don't call a screen.

The potential for calling a screen is greatest when the serve is low and fast and the receivers were prevented from seeing the contact of the serve, or if a player on the serving team moves to get between the server and the receiver after the receiver has moved to see the contact of the serve.

Case 10: Lineup Submission

If five minutes prior to the end of warm-up the umpire sees that the libero position is not marked on the starting lineup, it would be good preventive officiating to make certain the coach did not intend to use the libero for that game. If this is observed while checking the lineup with players on the floor, it would be too late for that team to be allowed to use the libero for that game. They may, however, add the libero to the lineup for the following game(s).

Case 11: Wrong Uniform Number

Because Richmond has a wrong uniform number listed for one of their players, they have supplied an inaccurate roster to the scorer. The roster should be corrected, and the first game begins with a loss of rally for Richmond's first serve and a point for Westwood.

Had the scorer discovered that Richmond had an unlisted team member, that player would have been ineligible until the coach added the player to the roster.

Remember, there is no penalty if an error is discovered and corrections are made before the deadline.

Case 12: Adding Names to the Roster

Independence committed two roster violations—the first for turning in its roster late to the scorer, and the second for trying to add names to its roster after the deadline. They should be penalized separately for each violation because the violations occurred separately. Therefore, although Independence was due to serve first, Centralia should serve first with a 2 to 0 lead.

Case 13: Changing Uniform Numbers

Yes, this is legal; the Jamestown player can reenter the game with a different uniform top and number. Jamestown should not be assessed a penalty for this. If, however, the Jamestown coach decided he wanted the player who was originally wearing #15 to play, and that player put on the uniform top of another player, then Jamestown would be penalized for that roster change.

Case 14: Number Mix-Up

Player #22 must replace player #12 on the court before the game begins. There is no penalty, as long as there is no delay of the game. Note that the Pittsfield coach doesn't have the option of leaving #12 on the court, even if she were to say she'd take a penalty for doing so.

Case 15: Libero Position

The libero must be replaced with the player the libero originally replaced. Because the libero was positioned in the front row, the serving team was out of rotation. The point that was awarded Ruthville for the ace should be canceled, and a loss of rally results. The oponent should get a point and the serve.

Case 16: Libero Setting the Ball

This is an illegal attack. An attack may not be completed while the ball is completely above the height of the net if it comes from the libero's overhead finger set while positioned on or in front of the attack line. The libero may not set the ball using overhead finger action while on or in front of the attack line extended, for a completed attack above the height of the net. Proper signal mechanics would be to signal an illegal attack followed by an indication to the libero as to the reason.

Case 17: Libero Serving

Rule 10-4 tells us only one libero replacement may be exercised per dead ball. There is an exception in the instance the libero, who is already on the floor, replaces the player that is about to serve. This is considered a double replacement as #5 (who was originally replaced by the libero) returns to the game and the libero is now replacing #10.

CHAPTER 8

PLAY

In the previous two chapters, you considered cases having to do with rules 1 through 7, covering the game, the court, equipment, uniforms, officials and teams. In this final chapter you'll make rulings in cases that have to do with the final five rules:

- Rule 8: The Serve
- Rule 9: During Play
- Rule 10: Substitution and Libero Replacement
- Rule 11: Time-Outs and Intermission
- Rule 12: Conduct

As in the previous two chapters, read each case, decide how you would rule, and then check your rulings against those at the end of the chapter, beginning on page 110.

Rule 8: The Serve

Rule 8 outlines the legality of play surrounding the serve, including re-serve situations, illegal serves and service faults. Consider how you'd rule in the following cases that focus on various aspects of serving.

CASE 1: Serving Before the Signal

Jamestown is playing Pittsfield in tournament play; other tournament games are being played at adjacent courts. Before you give the signal to serve, the Jamestown server, hearing a whistle from another court, serves. Pittsfield is not ready to receive serve, and the ball drops, untouched, on their side of the court. What is your call?

Would your call be different if the crowd noise were so great that it was difficult to hear your whistle? What if there were no noise problem or other whistles, but the server was just confused or overly excited and served before you signaled for serve?

CASE 2: Re-Serve Privileges

Player #7 on York is awarded a re-serve in a match against Brownsburg. She then serves two more points before she is replaced by #11. As #11 is serving, she is awarded a re-serve. Is this correct, given that the player she replaced had already been given a re-serve?

CASE 3: Missing a Tossed Ball

You signal the Centralia server to serve in a match against Westwood. The server, attempting a jump serve, swings and misses the tossed ball. How do you rule? Does he get a re-serve?

Would your decision be different in any of the following situations?

1. The server swings and misses, and the ball hits his shoulder.
2. The server tosses the ball, and then doesn't swing at it, but lets it drop to the floor.
3. The server tosses the ball, and then catches the toss because it was poorly executed.
4. The server tosses the ball, doesn't swing at it, and it touches his knee as it drops to the floor.

CASE 4: Serving Out of Order

In a game against Richmond, an Independence server has scored two points and is still serving when her coach realizes she is serving out of order. The coach calls a time-out. When the Independence players return to the floor after the time-out, the proper server—not the one who had been serving—serves, and Independence scores three more points.

At this point, the umpire realizes that a different player has been serving since the time-out. What should happen?

Rule 9: During Play

This rule covers a variety of issues, including court protocol, contacting the ball, multiple contacts, center-line play, the back-row players, net play and more. Read the following cases and decide how you'd respond in each situation. Then check your responses against those in the "Answers" section later in the chapter.

CASE 5: Block or No Block?

The CF on Brownsburg jumps to block a spike by a Jamestown player. The Brownsburg player jumps too early, though, and is on the way down when he contacts and deflects the ball. The point of contact is below the top of the net. How does this affect Brownsburg?

Would your response be any different if, in the same situation, the Brownsburg player contacted the ball while it was still partially above the top of the net?

CASE 6: Multiple Contact?
The Pittsfield RF, in attempting to block a York hitter's spike, deflects the ball into Pittsfield's side of the net. The RF reaches out to save the ball, which then bounces off her wrist and then her shoulder. Is this legal?

CASE 7: Stepping Over the Center Line
The Westwood RF spikes the ball for a point. After scoring the point, the RF steps completely over the center line. Does the point count?

Would your ruling be any different if the hitter had touched the net after scoring the point?

CASE 8: Illegal Back-Row Attack
In a game against Centralia, the Independence CB, who is in front of the attack line, sets the ball to a teammate. The ball is completely above the top of the net. Before the teammate can play the ball, it partially crosses the net, and the Centralia CF blocks it into the Independence CB. The ball stays on Independence's side of the net. Is there any call to make?

Would your answer change if in the same situation the ball rebounded off the Independence CB, crossed the net and fell untouched in Centralia's court?

CASE 9: Simultaneous Contact?
A York spiker and a Jamestown blocker simultaneously contact a ball that is directly above the net. Is this legal net play?

What if the simultaneous contact occurred when the ball was completely on the York side of the net?

CASE 10: Huddling Between Points
The Pittsfield players, in a match against Brownsburg, huddle after each rally before returning to their positions for the next play. This slows the tempo of the game, and you issue a warning to the Pittsfield captain.

However, Pittsfield continues to huddle after every point, slowing the tempo of the game. How do you respond?

Rule 10: Substitution and Libero Replacement

Rule 10 details the procedures of substitutions, including legal requests, the correct procedure for substitutes entering a game and the legality of play surrounding substitutes. Decide how you would respond to the following cases, and then check your responses against those at the end of the chapter.

CASE 11: Substitution Request

During a game against Centralia, the Richmond coach calls for a time-out and legally substitutes as soon as she is granted the time-out. At the end of the time-out, after all the players have returned to the court and before you signal for the serve, the Richmond coach requests another substitution. Is this legal?

CASE 12: Substitution Procedure

The Westwood coach stands and signals for a substitution in a game against Independence. The umpire recognizes the request. The coach then walks to the umpire and gives the number of the substitute and the player to be replaced. Is this correct procedure?

What if, instead, the coach did any of the following after being granted his request?

1. He immediately sits down.
2. He walks to the sideline within the replacement zone and talks with his substitute.
3. He remains at the officials' table and talks with the officials.

Do any of these constitute a correct response on the part of the coach?

CASE 13: Recognizing a Substitute

A Richmond substitute, about to enter a game against Jamestown, approaches the substitution zone. The umpire sees the substitute approach and blows the whistle before the player gets to the 10-foot line extended. Is this correct procedure?

Would your response be different if the umpire refused to blow the whistle until the player got across the attack line extended and was within 3 feet of the sideline?

CASE 14: Server Replaced by a Substitute

In a game against Pittsfield, an Independence server scores a point. He is then given a re-serve on his next serve, but instead of serving, he is replaced by a substitute. Is this legal?

What if he were replaced by a substitute after you had declared a replay?

Rule 11: Time-Outs and Intermission

This rule focuses on time-out requests, intermission procedures, the reviewing of officials' decisions, injury time-outs, and more. Try your hand at the following situations, and then check your rulings against those at the end of the chapter.

CASE 15: Time-Out Before the Match

Just as his team is about to begin its match against Brownsburg, the Centralia coach calls time-out. After the time-out, Centralia is still not ready to play, so you charge them with a second time-out for unnecessary delay. At the end of this penalty time-out, Centralia is still not ready to play. What happens?

CASE 16: Reviewing an Official's Decision

In a close game between York and Westwood, the York coach calls time-out and asks you to reconsider an illegal hit call. How should you respond?

Would your response be any different if the coach had asked you to reconsider any of the following?

1. A back-row player attack call, because of the height of the ball
2. A back-row player attack call, because the player was really the RF
3. A misapplication of a rule

CASE 17: Unnecessary Delay?

Jamestown and Pittsfield have just played the first game of their match. Jamestown returns to the court and is ready to play after two minutes have elapsed. Pittsfield is not in position to play, however, until three minutes have elapsed. Are they assessed an unnecessary delay?

Would your response change if Pittsfield were not ready to play until three minutes, fifteen seconds had gone by?

CASE 18: Libero Replacement Protocol

After the referee calls for serve, Jamestown's libero runs onto the court to replace the CB player. Would you allow the serve to continue?

Rule 12: Conduct

Coaches' and players' conduct—and that of spectators as well—is the focus of rule 12. Make your judgments in the following cases and see if you were correct by checking your rulings against those in the next section.

CASE 19: Coach Verbally Abusing Players

Brownsburg is not performing well in a match against York. Brownsburg had easily beaten York earlier in the season, and Brownsburg's coach becomes angrier and angrier as his players make poor passes and commit violations. As the match goes on, the coach begins to strongly verbally abuse his players, chastising the players on the floor, berating the players on the bench and cursing at their play. Should you do anything?

CASE 20: Conduct of Bench Players

In a match against Centralia, some of the Westwood bench players are standing in the warm-up area watching the game, while a few others are sitting on the floor in front of the bench. Is this OK?

CASE 21: Player Using Profanity

A Richmond player spikes a ball that a line judge calls out. You concur with the call. The player directs profanity your way in response to your upholding the call. Which of the following responses is incorrect?

1. You disqualify the player from the match for unsporting conduct and penalize Richmond with a side-out. You tell the umpire to inform the Richmond coach of the reason for the disqualification.

2. You disqualify the player from the match for unsporting conduct and expel the player from the gymnasium.

3. You disqualify the player from the match for unsporting conduct and direct the player to the bench area or to the supervision of authorized school personnel.

Answers

See how well you know rules 8 through 12 by checking your rulings in the preceding cases against those in this section.

Case 1: Serving Before the Signal

You should call for a replay. It was not the Jamestown player's fault that she mistook a nearby whistle, but because you had not signaled for serve, play cannot begin.

The same ruling would apply if the crowd noise made it difficult to hear your whistle, or if the server were simply confused or overly excited. In all three cases, call for a replay.

Case 2: Re-Serve Privileges

Yes, it's correct to award a re-serve to player #11, even though she replaced a player who had already been given a re-serve. Each player is entitled to one re-serve during the team's term of service.

Case 3: Missing a Tossed Ball

After the Centralia server swings and misses a tossed ball, you should give him a re-serve. In all other examples presented, you should give the server a re-serve—except in the case in which he swung and missed the ball and it hit him on the shoulder. If the ball had not touched him, you could have issued him a re-serve. He does get a re-serve in the case of the ball touching his knee after he allowed the ball to drop to the floor, because in that situation he didn't make an attempt to contact the ball.

Case 4: Serving Out of Order

You should cancel all points scored by both servers: the incorrect server who served before the time-out, and the correct server who served after the time-out. When the first serve was served by the wrong player, it should have resulted in a loss of rally. Therefore, Richmond should get a point and the serve.

Case 5: Block or No Block?

No, because the Brownsburg player contacted the ball below the top of the net, that counts as the first hit and Brownsburg has two more hits coming. This play is not considered a block, even though that's what the Brownsburg player was attempting. A block can't take place unless the player's hands are above the top of the net at point of contact.

If the Brownsburg player had contacted the ball while the blocker's hand(s) were still above the top of the net, this would have been considered a block and Brownsburg would have had three hits remaining.

Case 6: Multiple Contact?

Yes, it's a legal multiple contact (one attempt to play the ball). The multiple contact came on the first team hit. Had it been on the second or third team hit, it would have been an illegal multiple contact. Play should continue.

Case 7: Stepping Over the Center Line

The point counts. The hitter can step over the center line once she scores a point. The ball must be live for a line violation (or for a net foul) to occur. Thus, if she were to touch the net after scoring a point, the point would count in that case as well.

Case 8: Illegal Back-Row Attack

There is no call to make; this is legal. Play should continue with the next play by Independence being its second hit (the first hit being when the ball struck the Independence CB).

If the ball rebounded off the Independence player, crossed the net and fell untouched in Centralia's court, it would be a point for Independence on a back-row attack.

Case 9: Simultaneous Contact?

The simultaneous contact directly above the net is legal, and play should continue. If the ball were contacted simultaneously when it was completely on the York side of the net, it would be an over-the-net violation on Jamestown. (The offensive team must have the first opportunity to complete their attack.) The point would be awarded to York.

Case 10: Huddling Between Points

You should respond by penalizing Pittsfield for unnecessary delay. (In other words, they should be assessed, and given, a time-out. If they have exceeded their time-out allotment, then a loss of rally or point should be awarded to their opponent, and the game should be resumed immediately.) You gave them a warning and they didn't heed it. They need to be ready to play immediately after each rally. Don't allow a team to interrupt the flow of a match.

Case 11: Substitution Request

No, it's not legal. You should deny the request for the second substitution. A team is permitted only one substitution request during the same dead ball.

Case 12: Substitution Procedure

Of all the options listed, the correct response of the coach, once he has been granted his substitution request, is to sit down prior to the ball becoming live again. He shouldn't talk with the umpire or the officials at the table, but he may address the players provided he remains in the libero replacement zone, off the court, and returns to the bench prior to contact of the next serve.

   If the coach uses this time during the dead ball to talk to the umpire, that official should remind the coach to use the privilege of standing at his bench for coaching his players. If the head coach receives a yellow or red card, he loses this privilege and must remain seated for the remainder of the match except to request a time-out or substitution, ask the umpire during a dead ball to review the score, verify the number of time-outs taken by his team, greet a replaced player, confer with players during time-outs or attend an injured player with permission of the official.

Case 13: Recognizing a Substitute

The umpire is not correct in blowing the whistle before the substitute crosses the 10-foot line extended. The time the umpire should recognize the substitute is when the player crosses the attack line extended at the sideline.

Case 14: Server Replaced by Substitute

Once you declare a re-serve, the server cannot be replaced. A re-serve is considered part of a single attempt to serve, and the game can't be interrupted until after the ball is served. You should charge Independence with an illegal substitution for attempting to substitute for the server.

If the substitution came after you declared a replay, this would be legal. In this case, the substitute could enter and serve.

Case 15: Time-Out Before the Match

You should charge Centralia with unnecessary delay, give a point to Brownsburg and begin the game immediately.

Case 16: Reviewing an Official's Decision

You should not discuss the York coach's question about an illegal hit call; judgment calls are not subject to review. Thus, the question about the height of the ball during the back-row player attack is also not subject to review.

However, it is appropriate to discuss the other two matters because these are not judgment calls. If you determine that the back-row player was really the RF, or that some rule was misapplied, then correct the decision and resume play immediately, with no time-out being charged to York. If you determine that the play should stand as it was called, the time-out is in effect and York remains charged with it.

Case 17: Unnecessary Delay?

You shouldn't assess Pittsfield an unnecessary delay if they aren't ready until three minutes have elapsed, even if Jamestown has been on the court for a minute, ready to go. If both teams are ready to play before three minutes elapses between games, you can begin play, but a team isn't required to be ready to play before three minutes just because the opponent is ready.

If, however, Pittsfield wasn't ready until three minutes and fifteen seconds had gone by, you should assess them an unnecessary delay.

Case 18: Libero Replacement Protocol

The libero replacements must take place after the ball is blown dead and before the whistle (or signal) for serve. A replacement that occurs after the signal for serve is considered illegal alignment and results in loss of rally and point.

Case 19: Coach Verbally Abusing Players

You certainly should do something. You should administer, at the very least, a red card to the Brownsburg coach for unsporting conduct. You are not called to develop rabbit ears and hear everything on the sidelines, but in this case, because the abuse and misconduct are obvious and are detracting from the match, the coach should be penalized.

Case 20: Conduct of Bench Players

No, the behavior of the Westwood players is not OK. Players can be in the warm-up area to warm up before entering a game, but these players are simply observing the game from the warm-up area. Likewise, players shouldn't be on the floor in front of the bench. They should be seated on the bench, except when they are spontaneously reacting to a good play by their own team, or standing at the bench to greet a replaced player before immediately sitting down again.

Case 21: Player Using Profanity

Answer 2 is incorrect; you shouldn't expel the player from the gymnasium. It is correct to disqualify the player from the match, but you shouldn't insist that he be removed from the facility unless the player is under the direct supervision of authorized school or security personnel.

The disqualified player can remain on the team bench. It is the coach's responsibility to keep the player under control at all times. You should forfeit the match to the opponent if the disqualified player exhibits further misconduct. Remember that cards carry over from game to game throughout a match.

NFHS Officiating Volleyball Signals

Illegal alignment or improper server

Line violation

Illegal hit

Delay of serve

Over-the-net foul

Net foul or net serve

| Legal back-row attack | Illegal attack of serve or illegal attack | Illegal block or screen |

| Ball touched | Four hits | Double hit |

| Ball lands in bounds | Out-of-bounds or antenna violation | Begin serve | Authorization to enter |

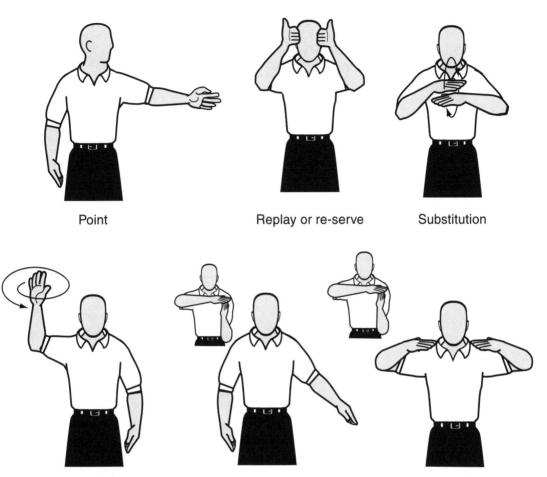

Point

Replay or re-serve

Substitution

Illegal
substitution

Team time-out

Officials' time-out

Unnecessary
delay

End of game

Change of courts

GLOSSARY

antennae—The vertical rods attached to the net over the sidelines of the court. The antennae extend three feet above the net, and the ball must pass inside the antennae when it crosses the net in order to be in play. If the ball hits the antennae or crosses the net outside of them, the play is over.

attack—Any action other than a block or serve that directs the ball toward the opponent's court.

attack line—A line on the court 3 meters from and parallel to the net on each side that separates the frontcourt from the backcourt. Back-row players are not allowed to jump and attack the ball from in front of the attack line. Also called the 10-foot line or the 3-meter line.

backcourt—The area between the attack line and the end line (from sideline to sideline) on each side of the net.

baseline—The line that marks the end of the court on each side of the net. Each baseline is 30 feet from the net and runs parallel to the net. Also called the *end line*.

block—When a player(s) close to the net prevents the ball coming from the opponent from crossing the net by reaching higher than the top of the net.

centerline—A line that runs parallel to and directly under the net from sideline to sideline, dividing the court in half.

coin toss—A decision protocol conducted during the prematch conference. The winner of the coin toss chooses either to serve or to receive. The home team designates its bench and corresponding court prior to the coin toss.

contact of the ball—A touch of the ball by a player, excluding a player's loose hair.

end line—The line that marks the end of the court on each side of the net. Each end line is 30 feet from the net and runs parallel to the net. Also called the *baseline*.

foul—A failure to play by the rules. Your rules book provides a more complete definition of fouls and their penalties.

let serve—A playable serve that hits the net without touching the antenna and continues across the net into the opponent's court.

libero player—A defensive player who plays only in the back row and who may replace any back-row player. These replacements may occur throughout the game and do not count toward the 18-substitution limit. This player may also serve in one serving position.

lineup—A list of the uniform numbers of the players in the game, placed in their starting positions on the court.

live ball—A ball in play; a ball is live from the moment it is legally contacted until it is declared a dead ball.

loss of rally—Occurs when the serving team violates a rule. The ball and a point are given to the opponent.

match—A series of games played at one time; usually consists of five games, but a state association may allow matches of three games. The winner of the match is the first team to win three of the five games, or two of the three games.

net—The equipment that divides the court in half and separates the playing areas for the two teams.

out of bounds—The area out of the court boundaries as defined in the rules book; a ball that falls out of bounds is considered a dead ball.

pass—A play in which the ball is hit into the air so a teammate can get into position to contact it.

penalty—The response to an infraction that is applied to the offending person or team.

penalty point—A point awarded to a team when its opponent commits a fault (violation).

prematch conference—A meeting conducted by officials prior to the timed warm-up, in which a coach and captain from each team are present for information pertinent to the conduction of the match.

rally scoring—A scoring system in which a point is scored on each rally that begins with the serve and ends with a dead ball, regardless of which team served. Matches consist of five games (state associations can adopt a three-game system if they choose). Games go to 25 points, they must be won by at least 2 points and there is no point cap. After 24 points, the first team ahead by 2 points wins the game. Deciding games are to 15 points, again without a point cap.

replacement—The act of the libero player replacing any player in a back-row position for the purpose of playing defense. Replacements are unlimited and are not counted toward the 18-substitution limit per team.

replay—The act of putting the ball into play (other than at the start of the game) without awarding a point or loss of rally and without a rotation for the serve.

re-serve—A situation that occurs when the server releases the ball for service, then catches it or drops it to the floor.

roster—A list of the names and numbers of all eligible players on a team.

screening—An illegal action by the serving team that prevents receivers from seeing the contact of the serve or the path of the served ball.

serve—The contact with the ball that initiates play.

sideline—The lines that mark the sides of each playing area. These lines are 30 feet long from the net to the end lines on each side of the net.

unnecessary delay—Any action by a team, player or coach that unnecessarily delays the start or resumption of a game.

warning—Notice given in the form of a yellow card for a first minor offense. No penalty is assessed, but the warning is recorded in the scoresheet.

INDEX

Note: The italicized *f* following page numbers refers to figures.

ABOUT THE AUTHOR

Officiating Volleyball was developed by the American Sport Education Program (ASEP) in cooperation with the National Federation of State High School Associations (NFHS). Based in Indianapolis, the NFHS is the rules authority for high school sports in the United States. Hundreds of thousands of officials nationwide and worldwide rely on the NFHS for officiating guidance. ASEP is a division of Human Kinetics and has been a world leader in providing educational courses and resources to professional and volunteer coaches, officials, parents and sport administrators for more than 25 years. ASEP and the NFHS have teamed up to offer books, CDs, and online courses for high school officials through the NFHS Officials Education Program.

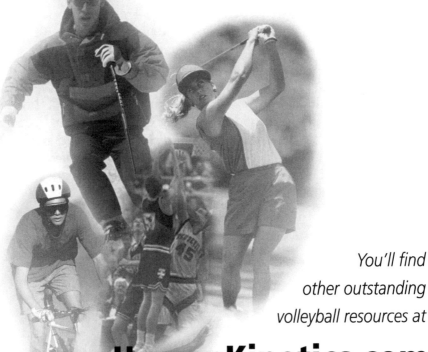